SEEKING GOD'S FACE

Seeking God's Face

Joseph Cardinal Ratzinger

WITH
The Lesson of the Christmas Donkey
by POPE JOHN PAUL I

Translated from the German
GOTTES ANGESICHT SUCHEN
by David Smith *and* Robert Cunningham

CLUNY
Providence, Rhode Island

CLUNY MEDIA EDITION, 2022

For more information regarding this title
or any other Cluny Media publication,
please write to info@clunymedia.com, or to
Cluny Media, P.O. Box 1664, Providence, RI 02901

VISIT US ONLINE AT WWW.CLUNYMEDIA.COM

ISBN: 978-1950970704

Cover design by Clarke & Clarke
Cover image: El Greco, *Apostle Saint Philip*,
between 1610 and 1614, oil on canvas
Courtesy of Wikimedia Commons

CONTENTS

PART I: MONTHLY MEDITATIONS

PART II: REFLECTIONS AT ADVENT AND CHRISTMAS

PART III: THE CONTRIBUTION OF ST. FRANCIS TO CHRISTMAS

PART I

Monthly Meditations

PREFACE

THIS SERIES OF MONTHLY MEDITATIONS was first published in 1976 and 1977 in the pastoral newsletter for the diocese of Aachen, Berlin, Essen, Cologne and Osnabrück. Insofar as these meditations are based on Biblical texts, they relate to those found in liturgical years B and C. In each case of a biblically based meditation, the letter B or C appearing after the relevant Sunday or feast day in the rubric below the title shows the cycle from which the Biblical text is taken. The length of each meditation was, of course, determined in the first place by the space available in the newspaper, with the result that I could do no more than hint at a great deal. But this may in itself be a help in stimulating the reader's own meditation. This is what ultimately matters in the long run and if I succeed in doing this then I will have carried out my intention.

Joseph Cardinal Ratzinger
Munich, Christmas 1977

THE MONTH OF JANUARY

The Morning of the New Year

In the Church's liturgy, New Year's Day is simply the eighth day after the birthday of our Lord, Christmas Day. The civil year is thus subordinated to the mystery of faith and its new beginning, and this points clearly to the way in which faith has transformed time. Without faith, our calendar is simply a way by which the revolutions of the earth around itself and around the sun are measured—it turns round itself in twenty-four hours and round the sun in three hundred and sixty-five days.

Days and years are mechanical factors in a cycle that repeats itself again and again. Time itself is circular and has no origin and no destiny. The earth follows its orbit without any concern for the sufferings and hopes of the people who inhabit it.

Time is transformed by faith. In faith, time is measured, not by the movements of the heavenly bodies, but by the acts of God, whose heart is, in all his activity, turned toward man. The two great events that are central in the movement of time according to our Christian understanding are the birth and the resurrection of the Lord. Our Christian feasts are based on our insight into these acts of God, not on our observation of the movement of the planets. The constant return of these feasts is qualitatively quite different from the endless repetition of the year from the first day to the last. It is not an eternally repeated cycle, but the expression of God's inexhaustible love, of which we are made aware by an act of memory. Unlike the beginning of the civil year, the Christian beginning—Christmas—has a very special newness. It offers us again and again the opportunity to return in the goodness of the God who became man, in that goodness to become a child again and in it to live a new life.

Let us now for a moment consider another aspect of this constantly new beginning of the Church's year. In accordance with the law of Israel, a child was circumcised and given a name eight days after he was born. The eighth day after his birth was the day of his legal reception into the community of Israel, its promise and the burden of its law. To be born biologically did not mean that the Israelite was fully born. Even today, full birth is not synonymous with biological birth. Man is not simply a biological being. Spirit, language, history and community all form an essential part of his being. He is, from the moment of his biological birth, in constant need of the others who surround him with their language, their history, and their community and its laws.

The eighth day in the life of Jesus was the day when he became legally a citizen, a member of his people. God became a member of this world and was given a name. This distinguished him as a citizen and as part of the history of our world and enabled us to name him as a person. When he became a living part of our history, the dark mystery of our own birth was completed; and our beginning, until then situated uneasily between blessing and curse, became a blessing. Since that time, he has been our sign—the Child who was born, who became a member of our world and who continues to take our history to God.

I would conclude with one further consideration. The eighth day is also the day of his resurrection and at the same time the day of creation. God's creation does not come to nothing. It is always moving toward the resurrection. The eighth day is therefore also the symbol of our baptism. It is the symbol of Christian hope as such—the hope that the resurrection and the life of the child are stronger than death. Our way is the way of hope. In the midst of passing time there is always a new beginning. This new beginning is eternal love.

"They Opened Their Treasures" (Matt. 2:12)

A Consideration of the Feast of the Epiphany

THE UNADORNED STORY of the adoration of the Wise Men at Bethlehem in Matthew's Gospel has had much less influence on Christians throughout history than the brilliant vision of the prophet Isaiah. Our modern representations of the crib simply reflect the essential elements of the Gospel account. In their details, they follow the bold outline provided by Isaiah. The dromedaries and camels and the wealth of the peoples come from him, and it is because of his vision that we see the greatness and beauty of the earth bowing down in front of poverty—the Child in the manger.

Is this, however, no more than a dream that has to give way to the sober reality of the situation as it was? We should not forget that the prophet was not depicting a single moment in time. On the contrary, he was describing a vision. Entire centuries are included in this vision, which gives us a glimpse into the distant future. Darkness and disappointment are overcome by the light that shines over the world from Zion, and the whole world goes on pilgrimage to the heart of Israel, which is trembling with joy in its unexpected luster.

But is this no more than a dream? Or is it perhaps not the truth? Does not in fact a light shine from the heart of Israel that continues to illuminate the world for centuries? The Magi of Matthew's Gospel are simply the first to make the great historical pilgrimage in which the greatness and beauty of this earth have been laid at the feet of Christ. The gold of the early Christian mosaics, the colored light from the stained-glass windows of our great cathedrals, the praise given at Christmas by the fir trees of our forests and the music of our voices and instruments— all these have been given to him in homage throughout history. Even the world's suffering has been offered to him and has found understanding and security in his poverty.

Nowadays, we have undoubtedly become a little puritanical. Should all these treasures not have been given to the poor, we ask. In asking this question, however, we forget that all the beauty that has been given to the Lord is really the only possession that is shared by the whole world. There is a great difference between stately homes and churches, between museums and cathedrals. What a contrast there is between working one's way through the Louvre, the Uffizi or the British Museum and going round a living church prayerfully praising the stones of its structure! The beauty that has been given throughout the centuries to the Child of Bethlehem is for everyone and all of us need it as much as we need bread. Anyone taking this beauty from the

Child to exchange it for something useful is behaving destructively—he is taking away the light that gives clarity and meaning to all our ideas and plans.

In joining the centuries-old pilgrimage in which all that is most beautiful in the world has been lavished on the newborn king, however, we should always remember that he is still living in the manger, in prison or in the slums of the Third World and that we are not praising him if we do not find him there. This awareness should not make us submit to a dictatorship of usefulness which outlaws happiness and imposes a somber seriousness. We should never try to separate care for the beauty of God's house and care for God's poor. We need both what is useful and what is beautiful. We must have not only our own house, but also the sign of God's presence in the world. Where God is glorified, our hearts are also bright. Where nothing is given to him, everything else drains away. Wherever his poor are excluded, he is not taken seriously.

"Your Sins Are Forgiven"

A Meditation on Mark 2:12 (Seventh Sunday in Year B)

IMAGINE FOR A MOMENT that the cure of the paralyzed man is a present event. The world is here and now lowering all those who are handicapped, injured or seriously ill through the roof of the Church and placing them at her feet: "You say that you offer men redemption. .." The Church might well reply: "I offer you the forgiveness of sins. I cannot make amputated legs grow again, but I can forgive sins."

The reaction of the modern world to this reply would be very different from that of the Pharisees in the original Gospel story. The world might well laugh in scorn and anger: "There is so much misery and suffering and you can find nothing better to do than forgive sins! You invented sin so that you would be needed to redeem men from it—from your own invention."

The Pharisees reacted differently. They were also angry and were quick to defend the honor of God who, they thought, was offended by Jesus' words: "How can he dare to speak as though he were God?" They knew beyond all doubt that there was a God, that sin existed, and that only God was able to forgive that sin.

It is precisely the existence of sin that modern man is unable to take seriously. Because of this rejection of the concept of sin, no one is directly touched today by the Gospel claim that the evidence of Jesus' divine nature is based on his power to forgive sin. Most people do not explicitly deny the existence of God, but they do not believe that he is of any importance in the realm of human life.

Hardly anyone seriously thinks nowadays that men's wrong actions may concern God so much that he regards them as sinful and offensive to himself, with the result that such sin must be forgiven by him alone. Even theologians have discussed the possibility of replacing the practice of confessing sin by conversations with psychologists, sociologists and lawyers. Sin does not really exist. There are only problems and these can be settled with the help of experts. Sin has disappeared and with it forgiveness, and behind that disappearance there is also the disappearance of a God who is turned toward man.

Is this really the answer to mankind's problems? Is this the solution for those for whom God is, as Sigmund Freud believed, no more than a universal neurosis, a sickness from which we are only now beginning to recover? Sin and forgiveness have disappeared, but something else has emerged to replace them—an excuse mechanism. Modern man has a permanent sense of guilt, but he cannot live with it, and, if the forgiveness by which this guilt is overcome no longer exists, then other ways have to be found of getting rid of it. It can, for example, be combatted. Many scientific methods for combating guilt have been developed in the twentieth century, and evidence of these can be found, for example, in the minutes of court proceedings. None of these scientifically based methods can prove that the terrifying effects of guilt do not exist, nor can they simply cancel out guilt and its effects. All that has in fact been done by these methods is to discover different causes for guilt.

One of the most notorious examples of the manipulation of this excuse mechanism is the attribution of all guilt to the Jews during the period of National Socialism in Germany. Since then, there has been a growing conviction that it is society that is guilty. We blame society now for everything. Instead of the God who forgives, we now have society, which cannot forgive and does not need to be forgiven, because it is guilt itself.

Does this excuse mechanism bring healing? No, it creates aggression. By placing guilt on a specific entity, it exposes it to attack. The anger that has held a whole generation of people in its grip can be understood in this way. This anger is directed against the society that is held to be guilty. But this externalized aggression does not set us free inwardly. In the last resort, it is a lie and we cannot live a lie. It would therefore not be wrong to say that this mechanism of excuses, however cunningly it may be disguised, is fundamentally no more than the art of lying, and, according to our present experience of it, the lie destroys men and the world.

In this situation, Christians can only turn to the Gospel, which can give us courage to grasp the truth. Only the truth can make us free. But the truth is that there is guilt and that we ourselves are guilty. It is Christ's new truth that there is also forgiveness by the one who has the power to forgive. The Gospel calls on us to accept this truth. There is a God. Sin exists and there is also forgiveness. We need that forgiveness if we are not to seek refuge in the lie of excuses and thus destroy ourselves.

If we learn how to accept this truth, then the second part of the Gospel story may perhaps prove its value in our lives today, since where there is forgiveness, there is also healing. We are forgiven and healed, like the paralyzed man. If we are just healed, the healing is in itself empty and meaningless. In the end, healing takes place only where there is also forgiveness and where God, in his love and mercy, gives man what he cannot always ask for, but what he so urgently needs.

Living in the Presence of God

A Meditation on 1 Sam. 26:2–23
(Seventh Sunday in the Year C)

IF WE ARE TO UNDERSTAND the theological significance of this passage in the Old Testament, we must first try to understand, at least to some extent, the two main actors in it—Saul and David.

King Saul is a tragic figure in the history of Israel. He was unable to preserve a good relationship with the priest and prophet Samuel, who exerted the most powerful spiritual influence in Israel. He was therefore doomed to fail. The political and military situation also continued to deteriorate during his reign and the popularity of the young and successful leader of his army, David, who was also Samuel's protégé, was increasing. Saul saw this rise of David's fortune as a threat and became more and more deeply depressed and obsessed with the illusion that he was being persecuted. He made several attempts to kill David, who had to become an outlaw. He was seriously compromised by this way of life as the leader of a band of robbers.

This was David's position when he came across Saul asleep and unarmed. Clearly, it would have been easy for him to seize power and become king. All that was needed was a single blow—Saul's own spear was close at hand. David must have been almost irresistibly tempted, but he did not heed the persuasive voices of his friends and Saul lived.

He did not act out of love of his enemy. His reasons for not having Saul put to death were in some ways even deeper. However inadequately Saul represented the authority bestowed on him by God, David stood in awe of that authority. Even greater was his fear of the ever-present power of God's justice.

This sense of God's presence is what singles David out so strikingly in the history of Israel. Despite his many and serious faults, he is shown again and again in the books of Samuel and Kings to have been impregnated with a deep and vital consciousness of the presence of God. For David, God was an all-powerful and decisive reality. God was there. His law was power. Success or victory achieved without him or against his will was failure, defeat.

David's fear of God's presence in justice sometimes strikes us as remarkable and unnerving, but it is never servile or unclean. It is also permeated with a profound trust in God's mercy. Whenever he was confronted with the choice of falling into the hands of his enemies or into those of God, David always unhesitatingly chose not the hands of men, but those of God, who was merciful even when he punished. The reality of God's presence was stronger for David, even in this story of his sparing Saul when the king was completely at his mercy, than the present reality of his own power. He only had to say the word to his friend or to draw his own sword, but he did not, because he knew that God was present.

This apparently archaic story may therefore have a deep meaning for us today. Both of the aspects to which I have referred apply to us too. David had respect for authority. I do not deny that we must be able to criticize authority. If this critical consciousness had not existed, Christianity would never have entered human history. But criticism is valueless if its criteria are merely plausibility and interest. Without respect, it is nothing. Democracy soon becomes anarchy and this rapidly deteriorates into a reign of terror and violence.

The second of the two motives preventing David from killing Saul is even more important for us today. Living in the presence of God means submitting all our interests to his justice. This brings us from the Old Testament at once to the Sermon on the Mount—the Gospel for today. All the individual statements made in that Sermon are images of the one decisive teaching—we must live, not on the basis of our own interest, but in the light of God's truth. If we do that, we shall be fulfilling the law and the teaching of the prophets and living under the new covenant.

The Temptation of Jesus

A Meditation on Mark 1:12–15
(First Sunday in Lent in the Year B)

MARK'S ACCOUNT of the temptation of Jesus in the desert seems at first sight to say almost nothing in comparison with the dramatic dispute with Satan that figures in the accounts of Matthew and Luke. Mark's text contains no reference to the controversy about the meaning of the Old Testament promises or redemption. It has a different function. Jesus' temptation was, for Mark, part of his fate as a prophet. From the time he was baptized Jesus was no longer subject to himself—he was subject to God's Spirit. He had been called by God and was henceforth led by the Spirit. He had ceased to be hidden and had begun his public life. He had become revealed, in the first place, it is true, only to become, in a sense, more hidden—entering the company of sinners who were waiting to confess their sins. He received the "sacrament" of those sinners, putting himself in their place. In anticipating the cross, he was also anticipating his resurrection and glorification. God's voice was heard at his baptism: "You are my beloved Son, the servant of God, representing many." The beginning and the end of his mission met here.

Jesus no longer belonged to himself. He belonged from this time onward to the Spirit. And the Spirit drove him into the desert as he had driven others who had borne witness to God before him. What is this desert? On the one hand, it was the place where God was encountered. Both Moses and Elijah had met God in the desert. God had shown himself to them when they were exposed to extreme poverty. God makes himself known not to the man who is satisfied, but to the hungry. On the other hand, the desert was also the place of temptation. Jesus was exposed to human nature in its most extreme form in the desert. The angels and the wild animals mentioned in Mark's text symbolize these two aspects of the desert.

Jesus left the desert with the wealth of the Word that increased in his silent and lonely meditation. He began to preach his message at the time of the arrest of John the Baptist. The tyrant could silence the witness, but not the Word. That continued to be heard more and more in oppression. What confidence!

In a concise and purposeful way, Mark gives us the essence of the Gospel message that the Church suggests for our meditation in Lent. It is that we are called, not to assert ourselves, but to conversion. What the Lord requires of us first and foremost is to be ready to change. He asks us to be foolish and not to conform to the normal attitudes of the society in which we live. In this way we are made free. It is in being changed and in penance that we discover the Gospel. The kingdom of God is to be found in our conversion.

If we consider this text as a whole, we are inevitably struck by its contemporary urgency. It addresses us directly and leads us to prayer and action. Almost automatically, Mark's account of Jesus' temptation in the desert, God's Word addressed to us, becomes our prayer to him. We pray that we may no longer simply serve ourselves, but learn how to be led by the Spirit. We pray that we may understand the mystery of the desert and that we may be conscious of the presence of the angels when we are being oppressed by the wild animals. We pray that the Word of God will continue to be preached and heard today and that we will continue to be confident in its victory. We pray that we too will bear witness to that Word. We pray that we shall be converted. And finally we pray that we shall in this way discover in faith and joy the Gospel of the Lord and the closeness of the kingdom of God.

God Suffers for Us

A Meditation on Gen. 15:5–12, 17–18
(Second Sunday in Lent in the Year C)

THIS TEXT IS ONE of the earliest in the Bible. Its main elements may well go back to the period before the Israelites took possession of Canaan. The mysterious imagery strikes us as pagan and it may seem to us presumptuous on the part of the Church to offer such a series of strange statements as a reading on Sunday. If, however, we go more deeply into these words, we shall see that they are quite closely in accordance with the fundamental theme of Lent—the mystery of the crucified Christ.

In the first place, the event that is reported in the passage is important enough. It describes the conclusion of a covenant between God and man. It is the beginning of that divine "testament" that was continued in Moses and was given a new and definitive form in Christ. This covenant with Abraham was concluded in a way that was fully in accordance with the customs of the period. Indeed, it represented the highest form known to man at the time of the sealing of an agreement—animals were cut in half and the partners in the contract passed between the halves.

This walking between the cut halves of the animals contained an element of curse. By doing this, the partners called down a curse on themselves if they broke the covenant. Their very lives were tied to the word that they had given. The gesture meant: what has happened to this animal will happen to me if I break this covenant; like them, let me be cut in pieces. Man thus bound his life to his promise. His word was more valuable than his life. In this way, then, the fundamental form of the faith of the martyrs can be seen in Abraham's act of faith. And that faith says: faith is valuable enough for me to suffer for it; faith is valuable enough for me to live and die for it.

This, however, is only one aspect of the Old Testament text, the easier one to understand. The passage goes on to say that Abraham sank into a deep sleep and the word used in this text is the same as that used (in Gen 2:21) to describe Adam's falling into a deep sleep when the woman was created. This deep sleep meant that Abraham (or Adam) became quite deaf to the world surrounding him. He sank down, going lower and lower into the depths of man's origin, the ground of all being. In these mysterious depths he became aware of something very remarkable and disturbing—something like a furnace and a fire was passing between the parts of the animals.

These were the symbols of God himself. God made himself present in an encoded form in the controlled heat of the furnace and the dangerous heat of the fire. He too was carrying out the rite of the oath and committing himself to this covenant. He too was ready to give himself entirely for the sake of this covenant and to vouchsafe for his faithfulness by his life and death.

This must strike us at first as at the worst monstrous and at the best absurd. How, we ask, should God suffer for man? How should he die? How can he link his fate to a promise made to an Israelite? The answer to this is: the suffering and crucified Christ. It was in Christ that the unthinkable became a reality. In Christ, God showed that man was worth suffering for. He revealed his faithfulness to man by letting his Son lose his life. Christ was torn to pieces like the animals. He became himself the sacrificial Lamb. In the passion of Good Friday, his body was torn apart and given over to death. God does not play with us. He has linked his fate to his faithfulness and in this way he has linked his fate to ours.

In Abraham's vision, the first station of the cross was, so to speak, driven into the ground of human history. We should consider what it means today and let our hearts be moved by it. It is surely good news that God should bind himself so firmly to his creature—to man, to us and to me. Can any power in the world seriously threaten us if he loves us so much? And should God's action not at the same time be an attack against our own indifference, but lukewarm faith? Should it not make us turn back to him?

Anointing for Burial

A Meditation on John 12:1–11 (Monday in Holy Week)

THE STORY of the anointing at Bethany gives the impression, when one reads it for the first time, of being no more than an anecdote. Yet Jesus himself regarded it as part of the Gospel: "Wherever the Gospel is preached in the whole world, what she has done will be told in memory of her" (Mark 14:9).

What, then, is the meaning of this event? Jesus himself provides an explanation in the words: "She has anointed my body beforehand for burying" (Mark 14:8; cf. John 12:7). Clearly, he was comparing what took place at Bethany with the anointing of kings and rich men at death. This anointing was an attempt to go counter to the event of death, in the conviction that death had not completed its work until the corruption of the body. As long as the body continued to exist, man was not completely dead.

Jesus therefore regarded Mary's gesture as an attempt to prevent his death. He recognized her helpless, but not insignificant concern—a concern that expresses love—to give life, even immortality, to others. The events that followed show clearly that no human concern, however strong, could ever purchase immortality. In the end, any anointing of this kind can only be an attempt to preserve the dead body. It cannot overcome death itself. There is only one anointing that is strong enough to meet death and that is the anointing of the Holy Spirit, the love of God.

There is, then, something that is both exemplary and lasting in Mary's anointing of Jesus at Bethany. It was above all a concern to keep Christ alive in this world and to oppose the powers that aimed to silence and kill him. It was an act of faith and love. Every such act can have the same effect.

Let me illustrate this with a sentence from the New Testament. John tells us that, when Mary anointed Jesus' feet, "the house was filled with the fragrance of the ointment" (12:3). This reminds me of Paul's statement: "We are the aroma of Christ to God among those who are being saved" (2 Cor. 2:15). The old pagan idea that the gods were fed by the aroma of sacrifices is changed here into the idea that Christian life enables the aroma of Christ, the atmosphere of true life, to be poured out in the world.

There is also, however, another idea that emerges from the story of the anointing of Christ. Whereas Mary was the servant of life in the Gospel, Judas was the servant of death—Jesus' death and his own death as the result of causing Jesus' death. Judas resisted anointing, the gesture of life-giving love, preferring the cold calculation of pure utility. At the deeper level, however, he was simply not capable of responding to Jesus or of learning from him how to understand the salvation of the world and of Israel in a new light. He had an already formed expectation of Jesus, which provided the basis of his appreciation of Jesus and which ultimately led him to reject him. Judas therefore represented calculation as opposed to love without any intention. He also represented man's inability to respond and obey as opposed to mature humility that lets itself be led in faith. "The house was filled with the fragrance of the ointment"—can we say that this also applies to us? Is our house full of the smell of selfishness, which is the instrument of death? Or is it full of the aroma of life, the life that comes from faith and is expressed in love?

THE MONTH OF APRIL

"The Lord Has Risen Indeed"

A Reflection on Easter Sunday

WHAT A SENSATION it would cause if we were to read one day in the newspapers that the remedy for death had been discovered. Ever since man has been on this earth, he has been looking for this remedy. We hope to find it, but at the same time we are afraid of it. The mere fact that, in one part of the world at least, our expectation of life has increased from thirty to seventy years has created almost insoluble problems.

Yet the Church proclaims that this remedy has in fact been found. Death has been overcome—Jesus Christ has risen and will die no more. What was possible then is also fundamentally possible and this remedy applies to all of us. With Christ, we can all be Christians and immortal. How can this be?

If we are to answer this question, we must first of all ask how it came about that Christ rose from the dead. The first answer that most of us would be tempted to give to this question is that he rose again because he was not just man, but also the Son of God. But he was undoubtedly also a real man and, what is more, he was also human for us. So we have to ask the second question: What was this humanity of Christ that was so closely united with God, the humanity that is the way that we should all follow? It was this: Jesus lived his whole life in contact with God.

Jesus lived in close contact with God. He spent his nights in prayer. Again and again the Bible tells us how he withdrew to be with the Father. According to all four Gospels, the crucified Christ died praying. His whole being was driven into God and transmuted into pure human life. Because of this, he breathed God's own atmosphere of love. Because of this too, he was immortal, being raised above death. We can see, then, how this should be applied to us. We have to unite all that we think, say and do with God's thoughts, words and deeds and in this unity seek the reality of his love. This is the way to immortality.

There is, however, another question that still has to be answered. What was the quality of Jesus' immortality? It was certainly not of the kind that men have sought since time immemorial in their search for the remedy against death. He was not, in other words, immortal in the sense that he did not die. An essential aspect of his history is that he died and that his immortality was a resurrection from the dead. What does this mean?

Love is always a kind of death. We die again and again in marriage, in the family, and in all our dealings with our fellowmen. The power of selfishness can be explained in the light of this experience. It Is a flight—an all too understandable flight—from the mystery of death that is love. At the same time, however, it is only this death that is love which is really fruitful. Selfishness of the kind that seeks to avoid this death impoverishes and empties us. The grain of wheat must die if it is to bear fruit.

Selfishness destroys the world. It is the gateway through which death enters and takes control. The crucified Christ, however, is the door of life. Death is the strongest power in the world, but it is not the ultimate power. In the crucified Christ, God has shown that love is stronger than death. Death is not victorious. Victory is with the Son, the living Christ. The more perfectly we follow his way, the more complete will be the victory in this world of his saving power over death.

"My Peace I Give to You"

A Meditation on John 14:23–29
(Sixth Sunday after Easter in Year C)

A SPIRIT OF PEACE emanates from Jesus' farewell discourses in the fourth Gospel. In them, he comforts his listeners as a mother comforts her children. He comforts the disciples at the hour of his departure. He comforts the Church throughout history—again and again the Church experiences the sorrow of his absence. His words do not provide us with a theory that enables us to understand the mystery of life, but they do provide us with a certainty by which we can live.

We should therefore be careful not to minimize the effect of these words, which touch the heart as much as the mind. We must try to understand them as perfectly as possible in order to become more deeply aware of the presence of the Lord who dwells in them. "My peace I give you"—what does it mean? According to appearances, everything contradicts these words. Since the Lord's departure, the world has continued to be without peace and not only the world, but also, unfortunately, the

Church, Christianity and the individual believer. What, then, can these words mean?

In the first place, we must remember that, in giving his peace to his friends, Jesus was simply bidding them farewell before going out into the darkness of the Mount of Olives. In Hebrew, the word *shalom* would have been used on such an occasion and we would translate this as "peace" or even as "salvation." A fairly close parallel is *adieu*, a form of farewell evolved in earlier Christian times and committing the person addressed to God's care and protection.

But this "peace" was also Jesus' last farewell before he set off on the way of the cross. It was more than a merely conventional word. Jesus, on his way to the cross, could not have been superficially wishing his friends an easy, comfortable existence in his absence. Nor could he, about to bring salvation to the world by experiencing the depths of human suffering, have been wanting his disciples to experience the peace of forgetfulness. No, it is clear from our knowledge of human psychology that real peace can only be brought by release from the captivity of comfortable lies and the acceptance of suffering. Repression is the most common cause of mental illness, and healing can be found only in a descent into the suffering of truth. Psychotherapists cannot, however, tell us what this truth is or whether it is ultimately good.

We can now go a step further. The two liturgical formulae, "The Lord be with you" and "Peace be with you" are interchangeable and for a very good reason. The Lord himself is peace. He did not simply use words when he took his leave of his friends. He who, on the cross, suffered and overcame the lie and the hatred of mankind was peace itself. He himself came through his cross and in giving his peace he did not simply give something— he gave himself.

These words, then, contain the Johannine reference to the institution of the Eucharist. The Lord gives himself to his own as peace. He places himself in their hands. As living bread, he unites the Church and leads men together into the one body of his mercy. We must ask him, then, to teach us how to celebrate the Eucharist truly and how to receive the truth that is love and in this way to become, through him, people of peace.

THE MONTH OF MAY

A Call to Spiritual Service

A Consideration of Acts 1:15–26
(Seventh Sunday after Easter in Year B)

THE PERIOD OF THE DISCIPLES began with the ascension of the Lord. From that moment onward it was their turn. They had to bear witness to the risen Christ and to take his word to the whole world. It is not surprising, then, that Matthias was called to be an apostle in the Church very soon after the Lord had ascended. Matthias is nowadays known as the patron saint of late vocations and this is, in a sense, what he is, but he was also the first to be called in the Church. He was certainly the first man to be appointed to a spiritual office by the Church and in the Church. It is clear, then, that Luke described his appointment as a model of a call or vocation, providing a norm for the Church throughout history.

What was the situation in which this call took place? The assembly that was to elect Matthias came from the Mount of Olives, the place where Jesus had suffered and been glorified. After having been scattered, the disciples were now able to pray together in one mind. There were one hundred and twenty of them, ten times the Twelve. They thus formed an apostolic community. The call occurred within the framework of the prayer of the elect. This was the first and most important condition—the call makes itself felt where the Church is of one mind and praying.

The second thing to happen was that Peter spoke. The representative of the Church's office acted. It was his task to take this initiative and to order the event. The third thing was his naming of the condition of the appointment, that the one elected had to be a witness to Jesus, had to have known him, and had to have had community with him.

The unique apostolate of the Church is therefore based firmly on the testimony of those who had seen Jesus both before and after his resurrection. This apostolate also has a lasting aspect. Anyone who wishes to be a messenger of the Lord must, even today, also have become his companion at table and his traveling companion. He must also know and love both the earthly and the risen Jesus. These conditions must be satisfied if we are to bear witness.

The next step is that the whole Church has to look for the suitable candidate, not by discussing, reflecting and deciding, but above all by praying that God will choose. This happened in Jerusalem after the Lord's ascension and it still happens in the Church.

Finally, lots were drawn. This strikes us as strange today, but it was the Old Testament way of handing a decision over to God when it went beyond the power of men. It is therefore possible to say that this procedure of drawing lots reveals the sacramental nature of the Church's office; no man can ultimately ordain another and place him in office, because it has come from a higher power, even though it is held in the Church by men.

The many different theological aspects of this structure of the call to spiritual service in the Church can therefore be seen quite clearly in this incident in the life of the early Church in Jerusalem. The whole Church, the apostolic office, the suitability of the candidate, and a new gift from God—all these factors must be involved. Above all, however, the Church of today should recognize that the place where its vocations have always been heard, both then and now, is still the same—the place of prayer and of unity and joy, the gifts that come from that prayer.

Life in the Trinity

A Meditation on John 16:12-15
(Trinity Sunday in Year C)

ON TRINITY SUNDAY this year, the Church gives us a Gospel that deals with the Holy Spirit and therefore also reveals the mystery of the Trinity. According to this text, the Spirit does not speak, as it were, from himself, but is a listening to and a making clear of the Son, who in turn does not speak on his authority, but is, as the one sent by the Father, his distinct presence. The Father also gives himself to the Son so completely that everything that he has belongs to the Son. Each of the three Persons of the Trinity points to the other two. In this circle of love flowing and intermingling, there is the highest degree of unity and constancy and this in turn gives unity and constancy to everything that exists.

These statements may perhaps strike us as very remote from the reality of our own lives and situated in the sphere of mystery. A moment's reflection should make it clear, however, that what we have here is a deep understanding of reality that reaches out to all areas of knowledge and touches all human decisions. If this vision of God is true, then the stable, consolidating and cohesive structure in our lives must be quite different from what we usually imagine it to be. What sustains us, in other words, is not the obviously firm and solid element, but the movement of the heart and spirit that leaves itself and is on the way to the other.

This attempt to explain the mystery of God by comparing it with the experience of man who was made in God's image is, of course, no more than an adaptation to our contemporary understanding of the original Gospel teaching. The evangelist's language is entirely trinitarian. What is more, because it is trinitarian, the Gospel text is—not additionally, but at the same time—also quite realistic and practical in what it says about the life of the Church and the way that the Christian should follow in the Church and the world.

The evangelist's discourse on the Trinity was not a speculation in the clouds without any purpose beyond itself. It resulted directly from a pressing need to answer questions asked by believers who were caught between the horns of an apparently insoluble dilemma. On the one hand, the Gnostics were confronting them with a modernization of Christian thought that was not based on Christ's teaching, but on their own. On the other hand, pious Christians were afraid to accept the advanced teaching of the fourth Gospel, which, in some ways, went much further than that of the synoptics.

These questioning Christians were told that the words of the historical Jesus could only be a beginning. The full scope of his teaching could only be revealed as it was explained and elucidated in the context of human history. This certainly applied to the first disciples and it has continued to apply to the whole Church throughout history, since it is the continuing process of the Incarnation of the Word.

On the one hand, nothing that is new can be said about Christ. God has no answer that is greater than himself. Christ is the definitive answer and, because he is definitive, so is the Church. This does not mean, however, that Christianity is inseparably linked to the past. There must be a living process of growth as the whole of mankind is involved in the Incarnation of the Logos.

This fundamental law of Christian life can also be applied to the individual, since it is only if each Christian makes his whole being available to the Word in the passage of time that time can as a whole be made open to Christ. Faithfulness and growth are not opposed to each other—they condition each other. Where there is faithfulness, there is also life. Where there is self-glorification, there is decadence.

The Trinity, then, provides us with the means by which both the individual and the community of the Church can disentangle the confusion of time. We shall not solve the problems that trouble us today by theorizing, but by spiritual means, by entering, in other words, into the form of the Trinity, based not on our own interpretation of this mystery, but on Christ's. The self-lessness of those who bear witness to Christ gives authenticity to the Church, just as Christ's selflessness bore authentic testimony to himself and to the Spirit. It is in this way that a living inter-relationship can develop, that growth can come about and that we can be led into the fullness of truth, a truth that is richer and greater than anything that we can invent.

THE MONTH OF JUNE

Corpus Christi

SINCE THE LITURGICAL MOVEMENT in this century has opened the way to a new understanding of the mystery of the Eucharist, many Christians have asked whether it is still meaningful to celebrate the feast of Corpus Christi in the traditional way. The true Corpus Christi seems to us today to be Maundy Thursday, the Christian passover revealing the authentic origin of the Eucharist and its proper orientation. Through his death and resurrection, celebrated at Easter, the Lord became our true life. This Lord, we are reminded at Easter, not only washes our feet as our servant, but also becomes our true bread.

All this is made clear in our celebration of the Easter event, and that Easter event is, of course, also celebrated at every Mass. Can the Lord's eucharistic gift be revered in any other way, then, than in the commemoration of Easter that occurs at every Mass? Can the mysterious call of the sacrament be answered in any other way than by receiving it, by being given it and thus giving oneself? Is the ostentation of the medieval feast of Corpus Christi really not a movement away from the greatness of the essential mystery?

Now, however, we may have reached the point where we can ask a different question: Has our eagerness to go back to the original experience perhaps not made us blind to the breadth and depth of Christ's gifts and to the many dimensions of the Eucharist? Is, for example, the Eucharist, as the Christian passover, not at the same time also the feast that is given to us by God? And surely feasting includes happiness, exuberance, going beyond the limitations of everyday experience and uniting the present and the future and heaven and earth.

Should there, then, not be one day in the year in which these feelings are expressed and the Eucharist is celebrated as God's feast, spreading out, as it has for so long in Germany, into the streets and squares and pointing to the world that is to come, where there will be no more temple, because the world itself has become the city of God? Surely there should be at least one day in which the streets become the scene not of business and haste, anxiety and work, but of joy and celebration that God is among us. This day of the Lord is at the same time the day of man, the day of the city, the village and the street. The street is, on Corpus Christi, fulfilling its highest destiny and serving as God's way to us and our way with and to God,

The liturgical renewal has rightly stressed that the Eucharist is not to be looked at, but received. But can we not add that part of receiving is to prepare a reception or a welcome for the Lord?

Surely the only proper way to receive the Lord is by going up to him as he comes to us and going with him as he goes with us. Can we receive him in any other way than by learning to look at him? We can only receive him by adoring him and in this way being at the same time infinitely separated from him and infinitely united with him. This kind of reception must also be a sensory experience if it is ever to be a spiritual one. In celebrating the feast of Corpus Christi in this way, medieval Christians may well have had a better understanding of the Eucharist than we Puritan Christians have today.

"For the Praise of His Glory"

A Consideration of Eph. 1:3–14
(Fifteenth Sunday of Year B)

THE ENTHUSIASM OF THOSE who had only recently been converted to Christianity and for whom being Christians was an unexpected gift and blessing from God emerges clearly from the beginning of the letter to the Ephesians. It is good for us to be aware of this. For us, Christianity often means a worried frown and almost a bad conscience whenever we feel happy to believe. We are afraid of triumphalism, with the result that joy has become a problem for us.

This passage is particularly joyful and it is so because the apostle dared to look at the very heart and center of Christianity—at the triune God and his eternal love. Anyone who nibbles around the outside of the reality of Christianity and never penetrates calmly and serenely to the center is always in danger of becoming increasingly absorbed by the often self-destructive process of critical reflection. We have to learn how to think and speak about the central reality of Christianity, however many preliminary questions are urgently raised, because in the end it is only the inner logic and beauty of the whole which flow from the heart of faith that can ever overcome the initial difficulties.

This text is above all an attempt to provide knowledge about the reason for being a Christian and the aim of faith.

We are not Christians because of our own achievement, but because God has sought us from eternity with the power of his love. The ideas of the preexistence of the Messiah, of the law, and the people of God were well known in Judaism. In this passage, the Apostle tells us that these ideas are true. In God's mind, we have been since eternity, because we belong to his Son. We therefore share in the Son's eternity and in the fact that he existed before all things. We are, as it were, already in him and God sees us in him, with his eyes.

We would do well to consider the meaning of this certainty of faith nowadays. We are living at a time when man is denounced as a naked ape or as a particularly treacherous rat and when he is regarded as the real mischief-maker who is destroying nature. Man is disgusted with mankind and fears his fellowmen. His hatred of the humanity in himself and in others is clearly growing.

Anyone who knows that God looks on him as a son has a certainty that is far stronger than this fear and hatred. He is certain of his origin and this is his answer to the pressing question of his destiny. The origin and destiny of man are described in the letter to the Ephesians in a number of closely related concepts.

The author speaks of redemption. He speaks of inheritance, by which he means that everything will belong to all men and that the world belongs to us. He speaks of the unity of the universe—everything in heaven and everything on earth—and of the removal of all opposites and of everything alienating. He speaks of undivided unity, in which all men and all things are in harmony with each other. This is redemption.

But how are we to be redeemed? Three times the author of the letter speaks of our being there for "the praise of his glory." The words recur like a refrain. This, then, is our way. If we dare to forget ourselves and to turn our faces toward our Creator, then these things will be ours—inheritance, unity and redemption. Surely the shining example of this simple truth is Francis of Assisi. If God is not praised, everything else collapses. It is only if we learn to turn our faces toward him again and break away from ourselves that we shall be redeemed.

The Power of Prayer

A Meditation on Gen. 18:20-32; Luke 11:1-13 (Seventeenth Sunday of Year C)

THE OLD AND NEW TESTAMENT readings for today present us with a teaching that would seem at first sight to be completely contrary to our usual understanding of the world. In the passage from Genesis we are told of a God who has dealings with a man, Abraham, and of a city whose fate depends on the outcome of the transaction between God and that man. This is as difficult to believe as the other idea that emerges so clearly from this story, that God can be made to give way by man's insistent pressure.

It is clear to us, in the light of our contemporary understanding, that the world continues on its way, following certain eternal natural laws. We can therefore only act for our own and the world's benefit by applying our natural reason to the situation; in other words, by discovering those laws and putting them at the service of man.

If, however, we look away for a moment from this ideal view of the laws of natural science and the application of modern technology to the world and consider our own experience of that other aspect of the world—its fragmentation, its inner contradictions, and its deep fears—we begin at once to doubt whether the world is really governed by immutable laws. Is there not also a great area of freedom, with its inevitable dangers and failures?

It is possible to understand the Old Testament text for today as soon as we begin to ask such questions. The essential meaning of this text is after all that the fate of a city—and indeed the fate of the world itself—depends on whether or not there is justice in that city—or in the world.

We can find evidence of this every day in our own lives, and it is impossible to deny that justice is of fundamental importance in the world and in all our dealings with our fellow men. On the basis of the Old Testament story, we can also go further and say that justice will be present in the world as long as man, like Abraham, continues to converse with God. Without God as our norm, there can be no justice covering the whole of mankind and the world. There can only be partial justice and group interests which do not consider justice as a whole. We can therefore say with conviction that, in such a situation, it is of essential importance for the world to converse with God and to be addressed by God.

This fundamental insight that is contained in the Old Testament story of Abraham's conversation with God is even more concretely presented in the Gospel for today. We must approach this text of Luke cautiously, since "Ask and it will be given you" seems at first to be almost a scornful remark. We should not, however, accept this statement at its face value. God is not simply giving something. He is not an idol who will take man's humanity away from him and change the world into a fool's paradise. What he gives is what he alone can give—the Holy Spirit (Luke 11:13).

God, then, gives the Holy Spirit. This is the gift of the Father to his children—the bread of God, by which we live. We have to ask God for the Spirit, because we need this gift and it can only be given by God.

It should now be possible to understand the parable of the persistent friend. It is, in other words, only if we persist with great patience in the presence of the silent God that we shall pray at all. Prayer is really no more than persisting with the silent God, possibly for a very long time. If we are to get to know someone, we have to share a piece of our life with him and continue sharing. In the same way, there can be no intimate prayer if we run to God with some need and then run away. We have to stay and knock, even though he may seem not to be listening. It is only if we are persistent that we shall become capable of recognizing the gift of all gifts—his gift of the Holy Spirit—when he gives it. It is only in this way that we shall become capable of asking for what God is so ready to give and of receiving it—the gift on which our life and the life of the world depend.

Finally, we shall also feel impelled by our gradual understanding of the words of this text to make the cry of the disciples our own: "Lord, teach us to pray." We need prayer. We live by prayer. But we cannot pray. You teach us to pray, Lord.

"All Generations Will Call Me Blessed"

A Consideration of the Feast of the Assumption of Mary

ELIZABETH GREETED MARY with the words "Blessed are you among women" (Luke 1:42) and the Church has continued to use the same words in addressing Mary. Even in the Gospel of Luke, the Hail Mary has the character of a prayer in which we hear not only the voice of Elizabeth, but also that of the early Church, the members of which went on greeting Mary in the form of a prayer.

In this scene depicted in the Gospel, the living veneration of Mary by the Church of the New Testament is made tangible and we can see that veneration of Mary is as old as the Church itself. According to Luke, it was inspired by the Holy Spirit, since the formula in which it is expressed is not a human invention, but something that was prompted by the Spirit of God himself.

If we read further in this passage in Luke's Gospel, we discover that the Church is given the task of honoring Mary, since it is clear that the words "Behold, henceforth all generations will call me blessed" (1:48) were addressed to the Church at all subsequent periods of its history. They contain a prophecy that is fulfilled in the praise given by Christians to the one who was especially favored by God.

In accordance with the familiar structures of New Testament thought, this call to the Church to give honor to Mary also points to the essential meaning of the feast of the Assumption itself. It is, in other words, not possible to call someone blessed if that person is in the kingdom of the dead. The God of the living is not glorified by the dead, but by those who live in him (see Mark 12:26ff.).

Luke made this statement even clearer by using two further literary devices. He characterized Mary as the remnant of Israel that was predicted by the prophets by the way he incorporated quotations from the Old Testament into the story of Mary's visit to Elizabeth and into the whole of the infancy narrative. She is presented in these accounts in person as the daughter of Zion who is called blessed and who ultimately emerges from all her testing experiences as saved.

Mary is also presented by Luke as the real ark of the covenant. She bears the living Word. As Augustine so strikingly said, before she became the mother of the Lord physically, she was already his mother spiritually. What is more, in the case of all the children of Adam and Eve, being born is a mystery of life which is at the same time also a mystery of death. New life presupposes the retreat of the old life into death. The birth of the one who is life itself, however, is in no sense an event of death. It is nothing but life. The ark of the covenant is incorruptible.

There are many parallels between the ark of the old covenant and the ark of the new. Let us just consider one—David's dancing before the ark (2 Sam. 6:14). This is paralleled by the unborn John the Baptist, who leaped for joy in his mother's womb, dancing, in other words, before the true ark of the Lord, when Elizabeth visited Mary (Luke 1:44).

Part of our faith is the joy that we experience in the Word made flesh. We are happy and dance in front of the ark and repeat Elizabeth's words: "Blessed are you among women and blessed is the fruit of your womb."

The Lowest Place

A Reflection on Luke 14:1, 7-14
(Twenty-Second Sunday of Year C)

JESUS' TEACHING in today's Gospel would seem at first sight to be no more than a piece of worldly wisdom or a page from a secular book of manners in which the reader is advised to follow an exaggerated form of modesty. In fact, however, Jesus' words about the highest and the lowest places are really a sarcastic instruction in the manners that should be observed when people tend to push forward without consideration for others. Manners or good behavior cannot be separated from Christian morals, since Christianity cannot succeed where ordinary humanity is absent. This is why Christian teaching has always had to take into account the human foundations of Christian life. In this sense, Christianity is firmly in the tradition of the Old Testament wisdom literature. In this text, we have an attempt to make man more human and to present him with a way of conforming more fully to God's will by coming closer to the human norm.

The Biblical authors always had the task of trying to prevent human manners from becoming purely external and of making them deeper and more central in man's life. This is clear from one of the wisdom books of the Old Testament, Ecclesiasticus, whose author, Jesus Sirach, speaks, in his instruction about good behavior, of the contrast between pride and humility and between self-glorification and readiness to love others.

In the parable about choosing places at table, Jesus taught at the deepest possible level. The wedding feast at which the guests try to claim the best seats without regard to the others present becomes in the Gospel a parable of the history of the world, in which a ruthless struggle for power has always taken place with little thought for the fate of others. God, who entered human history in Jesus Christ himself, does not participate in this struggle. All his life, from Bethlehem and Nazareth to Golgotha, Jesus took the lowest place. What he says in this parable is verified in the whole of his life and suffering. He was always on the side of the lowest and the last; and through him those who are the lowest and the last become the highest and the first. Indeed, he became so completely identified in his life and teaching with the lowest place that he has made himself present with us, not only in the Eucharist, but also in the least of men: "I was hungry and you gave me food, I was thirsty and you gave me drink, I was a stranger and you welcomed me.... As you did it to one of the least of these my brethren, you did it to me" (Matt. 25:35, 40).

These words of the Lord take us further and further into the heart of Christian life. The story begins with ordinary manners, which form the point of departure. The next step is that we have to learn not to reduce manners to an empty and dishonest structure, but to give them an inner content and meaning. When we have done this, we can move on to community and then to unity with the lowest and the last who is really the highest and the first, the Redeemer.

The one who invites us to his table to share in the Eucharist wants to lead us to a more and more completely eucharistic life. In this way, we shall find him more and more easily on the way of everyday life and thus be also on the way toward his eternal wedding feast, where those who are lowest and last will be forever the highest and the first.

THE MONTH OF SEPTEMBER

The Birthday of Mary

MARY'S BIRTHDAY is exceptional among the feasts in which honor is paid to saints, in that the Church usually does not celebrate the day of birth. The Church's practice was quite different here from that of pagan Greece or Rome, where the birthday of a great man—a Caesar or an Augustus, for example—was celebrated with great pomp as a day of redemption. The Church always argued that it was premature to celebrate a birthday because the rest of the life of the person born on that day was subject to such ambiguity. It was, in other words, impossible to predict the answers to certain questions simply on the basis of a person's birthday. Would his life really be a reason for celebration? Would the person who was born really be able to be glad about the day that he came into the world? Would the world be glad that this person had been born or would it curse the day that he was born? For twelve years, Germans had to celebrate the birthday of the Führer who was to save their nation, but the world came to curse this German leader as one of the most bloodthirsty tyrants of all time. No, the Church has always celebrated the day of death, believing that it is only possible to celebrate a person's life when he has passed beyond that life into death and judgment.

The Church recognizes only three exceptions to this basic rule, or rather, one exception and two others who are so closely connected to this one exception that their birthdays are also celebrated along with that of the single exception—Christ himself. There is no ambiguity about Christ's birthday, only praise: "Glory to God in the highest!" We can only celebrate with total conviction the birth of the one who, as God, became man and whose birth was based on pure love. What is more, the birth of this man who was God is also the cause of real joy and celebration, putting an end to any lingering fear that life is just the plaything of death and, even in its joyful moments, no more than a mockery of joy. It is this man who was born in Bethlehem and this man alone who has given our lives meaning and hope of fulfillment.

The birthday of John the Baptist is also celebrated by the Church because he was so intimately associated with Jesus. He was born in order to light the way for Jesus, whose birth was the inner reason for John's birth. The other exception is the birthday of Mary, Jesus' mother, without whom Jesus could not have been born. She was the gate through which he came into the world and not simply the external gateway. She had already conceived Jesus in her heart before she became his mother according to the body, as Augustine so meaningfully said. Her soul was the space from which God was able to gain access into humanity. Unlike the great and mighty ones of this earth, Mary, the believer who bore the light of God in her heart, was able to play her vital part in changing the very foundation of the world. The world can be truly changed only by the power of the soul.

The Imitation of Christ in the Sign of the Cross

A Meditation on Mark 8:27-35
(Twenty-Fourth Sunday of Year B)

"IF ANY MAN would come after me, let him...take up his cross" (Mark 8:34). It is worth recalling the very vivid legend that grew up around the historical event of the feast of the exaltation of the cross. The Byzantine Emperor Heraclius, the legend tells us, seized the cross from the Persians who had removed it from Golgotha and took it back himself to its original site in a triumphal procession. Carried aloft, the cross was decorated with the insignia of a world conqueror. When he reached the gate of the city, he suddenly found that he could walk no further. The Bishop of Jerusalem told him: "Emperor, with all this triumphal ornamentation that surrounds the carrying of the cross, you are not imitating the poverty and lowliness of Jesus Christ." The Emperor stripped off his lavish garments and was at once able to continue on the way of the cross.

The message of this legend is unmistakable. Whoever wants to imitate Christ must in one way or another get rid of all ballast.

For a time, it is often possible to live a Christian life in apparent harmony with the world and without obvious problems. But sooner or later, everyone reaches the gate and can go no farther. Everyone arrives at the point where he has to make a decision, either to accept a radical break in his life and strike others as absurd or to throw the cross away.

I was asked a little time ago whether the Christian was not inevitably confronted with an absurd alternative. Either he has to compromise for the sake of others and thus become less sincere or else he is consistent in his Christian life and thus becomes isolated, an emigrant and finally resigned.

A certain emigration is indissolubly linked with the mere fact of being a Christian. This situation goes back to Abraham, our father in faith, who was only a *paroikos*, one who dwelt alongside and did not really belong, an alien, in the land of the future. Our word "parish" is derived from this word *paroikia*, and it should still have the same meaning for us as it had for Abraham. We should remember that we are strangers or aliens because of our faith and not let this idea be obscured by the theological concept that is so popular nowadays, that of the community of believers.

We should therefore recognize quite clearly that it is not possible to be a Christian without contradiction, in other words, without a parochial element. We have to accept this fact, in the knowledge that any idea of openness to the world in which this element of contradiction is ignored cannot be supported either by Biblical evidence or by conciliar statements.

There is, however no need for Christians to be resigned passively to his fate. It is only if we refuse to conform to the spirit of the age that we shall be really free, mature and fruitful in our lives. The future is open to those who resist subjection and live as strangers. The reality of the promise contained in today's Gospel can be seen expressed in the lives of a handful of the saints whose feasts are celebrated by the Church this month: Gregory the Great, Hildegarde of Bingen, Stephen of Hungary, Nicholas of Flue. "Whoever loses his life for my sake...will save it" (Mark 8:35)—these words hold good not only for the life to come, but also for our lives in this world.

THE MONTH OF OCTOBER

Francis of Assisi

THE PRESSING QUESTION during the recent year of St. Francis was, of course: Has the greatest of all medieval saints anything to tell us in the present century? During the lifetime of St. Francis himself, many Christians were hoping for the emergence of a Church of the Spirit, in which a better, more pure, and more perfect form of Christianity would be expressed. They also believed that this renewed Church would lead the way to a radical change in human history.

Francis seemed to many such Christians, who were disappointed with institutional Christianity, to be God's answer to their expectations; and certainly the Christianity of the Spirit for which they were longing had seldom been manifested in a human being so strikingly as it was in him. But equally striking was the emphasis that Francis placed on obedience to the word of the Bible. His new principle was to hear the Word of God without explanations and therefore without the accompanying factors that might render it harmless. This principle was extremely upsetting for those who, with lukewarm casuistry and academic sophistry, reduced the Bible to an object of controversy far removed from the everyday life of the people of God. Francis heard God as he spoke to him quite personally through Scripture. His interpretation of God's Word was as literal as his obedience to it.

But this was the miracle of St. Francis—and it can be a miracle for all of us—that the Word of God accepted quite literally is also the spiritual Word. The Spirit appears, not in contradiction to the Word, but in the Word and the more deeply we penetrate into the Word the more clearly it appears. The Spirit does not come because we hide away from his coming behind barriers that we erect ourselves. We do this, of course, because we are afraid of being burnt by the fire that we sense is contained in the Word. Francis dared to accept the Word without the barrier of explanations and we should do the same now. We should receive it as a call to go in the direction of a living Christianity of the Spirit for which we too are longing.

Nowadays, too, we are interested in Francis of Assisi especially as a lover of animals and as the patron saint of those who are concerned with the conservation of our natural environment. In our greed, we are stripping the world more and more of its natural resources, and our concern to protect nature is certainly both good and necessary.

Many of those most concerned in this work, however, are seriously mistaken in the emphasis that they place on man in this question of conservation. They see man as the only real mischief-maker who is exclusively responsible for upsetting the peaceful balance of nature. Much of what they say points to a scornful attitude toward man and a desire to limit his spirit.

Francis' attitude toward man and nature was quite different. The seraphic idea of man, in whom the creature learns to soar and to sing, to transcend itself and to give of itself, was fulfilled in him. Whenever that happens, the deepest longing of the creature is expressed and its hidden sadness is transmuted into confidence and joy. Nature will not be saved by denying the Spirit. Man will only learn to respect nature if the Spirit of God is set free in him in a gesture of pure love.

The Healing of the Leper

A Consideration of 2 Kings 5:14-17
(Twenty-Eighth Sunday of Year C)

THE EARLY CHURCH FATHERS regarded the story of the healing of the Syrian Naaman, who suffered from leprosy, as a prefiguration of the sacrament of baptism. Naaman was rich and successful, at the height of his career as the leader of his king's army, when he was suddenly struck down with leprosy. He was condemned to a living death in which he had to watch his living body become corrupted; and, while he was still alive, he had to experience death.

Because of his leprosy, in which he was living in the grasp of death, he was also outlawed from his fellowmen. Not only in Israel, but also in all probability in all other societies of the period and place, the leper was not allowed to enter the sanctuary or to associate with other members of the community, whom he would make unclean. Isolated in this way, Naaman was handed over to the power of death, which was in itself the loneliness, ruin and destruction of society as a whole.

In this terrible time, when he was looking into the abyss of nothingness, Naaman seized hold of a straw—something that he had heard from an Israelite girl who was one of his wife's servants. According to this girl, there was a man of God in Israel who had the gift of healing. He therefore went to see Elisha.

The whole experience was, however, threatened with failure just as it was about to be fulfilled. Naaman was held back by his pride from doing what the prophet had told him to do—bathe in the Jordan. One of his servants then reminded him that he was no longer in a position to rely on his own important status in society. Confronted with death, he was no more than any other man and had to go to any extreme. It is clear, then, that it was not the Jordan that healed Naaman, but his obedience. He had to divest himself of his status and the pride that accompanied it and go down into and give himself, naked and unprotected, to the living God. His total obedience was the bath that purified and saved him.

The connection between Naaman and ourselves is surely obvious. Many of us—perhaps all of us today—are, like him, alienated, rejected, without human contact and condemned to a living death, at least at certain times in our lives. We are then placed in a situation when we are ready to seize hold of any straw that offers healing. We are, however, more ready to do "some great thing" (2 Kings 5:13) than something obscure and ordinary. The Church is too old and too unspectacular. The Church cannot heal us. This, then, is the decisive element—we should be ready to accept what is obscure and ordinary and to immerse ourselves in the water of obedience.

But this is not quite the end of the story. Naaman was healed, but another crisis was required before he was definitively saved. He wanted to show how grateful he was and could only do this, as a rich, powerful man, by offering money. But he had to learn that more than this was required—not his status, but himself, not money, but his lasting conversion to the God of Israel.

He took some of Israel's earth back with him to Syria and this many strike us as pagan, but it expresses a deep reality. The one God of Israel was not a philosophical construction. He was a God who was mediated by earthly means. This one God was for Naaman as he is for us the God of Israel. Naaman was converted in the most concrete possible way by receiving the God of that place, Israel. The same applies to us today. We can only truly honor the one God by being bound to the earth of the Church. He is the God who has accepted our earth into his eternity in Jesus Christ and has in this way overcome death.

Christ the King: I

IT IS ONLY ABOUT fifty years ago that Robert Eisler shocked the world of Biblical scholarship with a book in which Jesus was firmly placed among the figures in Jewish history whose aim was to realize the Davidic hope by bringing about the kingdom of God by means of political force. Eisler based his argument on two important events in the history of Jesus. These were the entry into Jerusalem and the cleansing of the temple.

The entry into Jerusalem, Eisler argued, could only have taken the form of a putsch or a surprise attack, leading to a seizure of power, and the cleansing of the temple could not have taken place among Oriental cattle dealers without violence. Fifty or so years ago, Eisler aroused only disbelief with his book *Messiah Jesus*. Today the spark that he struck has set men's minds alight. The Son of God, who did not change the world and who has nothing to say to young people who are deeply disturbed by the misery of mankind, has become Jesus the symbol of the struggle against oppression and the permanent revolutionary thorn in the flesh of the world.

Was Jesus' life, then, nothing but a failed attempt to seize the throne of David? Has the Church completely misunderstood Jesus' revolutionary intention and become reconciled with power?

Jesus entered the holy city on a donkey which did not even belong to him. He did not own a donkey himself. In so doing, he made use of a prophecy from the book of Zechariah which must have been well known to his own people (9:9): "Rejoice, greatly, O daughter of Zion...your king comes to you...riding on an ass...." Horses, which at that time symbolized military power, would disappear. The true king of Israel would not come on a horse. He would not be involved in the struggle against worldly powers. He would not try to seize power for himself. On the contrary, he would ride on a donkey, the symbol of peace, the animal ridden by the poor and valueless from the military point of view.

Jesus' entry into Jerusalem on a borrowed donkey is the symbol of impotence in the world and the fulfillment of the prophecy made by Zechariah and the promise made by God. As for the cleansing of the temple, such an attempt to assume power by violent means would soon have been crushed. For Jesus, it was above all a graphic prophecy of his death: "Zeal for thy house will consume me" (John 2:17). Jesus did not draw his sword. He did not speak any revolutionary words. His disciples died as martyrs for peace and were precisely in this way his witnesses. They testified to who he was and who he was not.

What, then, is Jesus' kingdom? The borrowed donkey is an expression of earthly impotence and of complete trust in God's power. That power is represented in Jesus himself. He did not set up his own kingdom alongside the kingdom of God. He simply bore witness to God's kingdom. His nothing, we might say, is his all. He stands not for earthly power, but for truth, justice and love. He stands, in other words, for God. The kingdom of God continues to exist in the world as something that can easily be broken. But it is only because of the kingdom that the world can be human. Revolutions do not make the world a human place, nor do revolutionaries, however good their intentions may be. They only leave bloodshed and violence. What enables men to live in this world are goodness, truth, faithfulness, and the certainty that God is himself all these qualities. What enables us to go on living is the faith that God is like Jesus Christ and that Jesus Christ, the man on the borrowed donkey, is the true king, the true and ultimate power in the world. Today, on the feast of Christ the King, we are asked to lead our lives in the direction of that power—"thy kingdom come."

Christ the King: II

THE FEAST OF CHRIST THE KING is of very recent origin, but its content is as old as Christian faith itself. The word "Christ" is, after all, simply the Greek translation of "Messiah," the anointed one or king. Jesus of Nazareth, the crucified son of a carpenter, was so much a king that the title "king" became his name. When we call him Christ, we are at the same time calling ourselves the people of the king, people who recognize him as their king.

What, then, is the kingship of Jesus Christ? We can only understand this properly if we go back to its origin in the old covenant. What strikes us at once in the Old Testament is that God did not in the first place want Israel to become a kingdom. The kingdom in fact came about as the result of Israel's rebellion against God and the prophets and the people's ceasing to do his will. After the tribes had taken possession of the land of Canaan, they joined together in a kind of confederation to form a single people without a ruler as such, but with a so-called judge. This judge did not, like a ruler, have the task of creating the law himself. His function was to carry out the law that had been given. Israel was in fact ruled exclusively by the holy law of God that had been handed down. Israel's king was in fact this law of God and therefore, through the law, God himself. All Israelites were equal and all were free because there was only one Lord, God, and he ruled Israel in the law.

Israel, however, became jealous of the people in the environment with their powerful kings and wanted to be like them. Samuel told the people forcibly that if they had a king, they would become slaves, but he was not heeded. They did not want freedom or equality or any of the elements that a kingship of God would bring. They wanted to be like their neighbors. In a word, they became like Esau, following desire and vanity rather than election by God. In the first place, then, the kingdom of Israel was an expression of Israel's rebellion against God's rule. In wanting a king, the Israelites threw away their election and became like the other people.

What is really remarkable, however, is that God consented to Israel's desire for a king and even provided an opportunity for that kingship to be renewed and fulfilled. Jesus was himself the son of David, the king. God entered mankind in him and espoused the cause of mankind in him. If we look more closely at this question, we can see that it is the fundamental form of God's activity with mankind. He has no rigid plan that he has at all costs to carry out. On the contrary, he has many different ways of seeking man out and finding him. He even makes man's devious and wrong ways into ways leading to him. This is clear, for example, in the case of Adam, whose very sin was made a happy sin in the second Adam, Christ, and it is clear in all the twisted ways of human history.

This, then, is God's kingship—a rule of love that seeks and finds man in ways that are always new. For us, this means a trust that cannot be shaken. God rules as king over us still and, what is more, he rules over each one of us. None of us should be afraid and none should capitulate. God can always be found. The pattern of our own lives should also be like this—we should always be available, never write anyone off, and try again and again to find others in the openness of our hearts.

Our most important task is not to assert ourselves, but always to be ready to set off on the way to God and to each other. The feast of Christ the King is therefore not a feast of those who are subjugated, but a feast of those who know that they are in the hands of the one who writes straight on crooked lines.

The Woman and the Serpent

A Reflection on Gen. 3:9-15
The Feast of the Sinless Mother of God (Year C)

GOD'S CONVERSATION with Adam and Eve when he expelled them from paradise points to the situation in which all of us are placed. We run away from God and hide, like Adam, from him and from each other. We live in fear. The serpent, which man feared, according to the judgment pronounced in verse 15, represents the dangerous element in life on earth and man's state of being threatened and exposed to danger. It also points clearly to the power of death which can strike us at any time or place. We try to trample on it, but cannot master it.

Death is still powerful, despite the power that we have gained over the world as a result of our scientific knowledge. The snake bite of death still threatens us, although from a new direction—that of the very technology that aims to protect us from natural dangers.

The Biblical author saw the serpent as the symbol of the power of sin, opening the door to death. We are not nowadays very alert to this connection between sin and death, and even Christians are often skeptical of this teaching, in the belief that God would not be so petty. It might, however, be to our advantage, in view of the distress that is so apparent today in society, to reconsider this link between sin and death. It is obviously very difficult indeed for man to remain constantly at the summit of his humanity and he is again and again tempted to seek refuge in idleness, corruption and intoxication. Whenever there is a breakdown in morality, man becomes disgusted with his humanity and ceases to understand and accept his fellow men.

Christians have traditionally understood God's pronouncement of judgment in Genesis 3:15, in which the distress of mankind is so vividly portrayed, in the light of faith as a promise. The perspective of despair is again and again transformed in the light of that faith into a perspective of hope and this is precisely what has taken place in the Christian interpretation of this text.

In the Old Testament text itself, the future is not clear. It is not possible, on the basis of the text itself, to know with certainty whether there will ever be victory in the alternation of trampling and biting between the woman and the serpent. The statement gained an entirely new meaning, however, with the resurrection of Jesus Christ and a new dawn emerged from the mists of twilight. It became quite clear that the ultimate victory would not be the biting of the serpent, but its being trod underfoot. Death would be defeated and life victorious. The sentence of death on man has, in other words, been transmuted into the messianic message or the "protovangelium" in the Christian tradition. In this first or "proto" Gospel, the woman—Mary—is really the "mother of the living" and the serpent has no part to play.

This story, then, is very suitable for Advent. How frequently we are tempted to despair of mankind! Man is often compared today to a filthy cesspool and even what is good in him is said to be illusory. This despairing view of man can only be refuted by the man or woman who is quite pure, who is without sin, and who is therefore the door through which God is able to enter the world and thus become one with mankind.

In the light of Mary's life and function, it is certain that man is not simply a repellent egoist. He is open to God. Mary's whole life can be summed up in the words: "Let it be to me according to your word." In thus surrendering to the will of God, she passes on to us the fruit of the tree of life, thus overcoming the gesture of Eve, who turned to the tree that was a "delight to the eyes" (Gen. 3:6) and yielded the fruit of death.

We are situated between the two trees, between the two kinds of fruit, that of life and that of death, and between our autocratic knowledge based on the "delight to the eyes" and the opening of our hearts and minds to God's word. If we believe, we will go in the direction of the story of the trampling of the woman and biting of the serpent and from there to Mary's consent to God's will and finally to the state where God's judgment becomes our salvation and eternal life.

"And All Flesh Shall See the Salvation of God"

A Meditation on Luke 3:6; Isa. 40:5
The Second Sunday in Advent (Year B)

IN ALL FOUR GOSPELS, the story of Jesus is closely identified in its opening with that of John the Baptist. This close unity between the Old and the New Testament was a fundamental aspect of the evangelists' understanding of the one history of God's dealing with men. John the Baptist, the last of Israel's prophetic figures, summarized in his person the way of the old covenant, embodying both the law and the prophets and representing the whole of the way that God went with his people. He, as it were, placed the torch of the Old Testament at Jesus' feet and handed over to him the part of the prophet, because everything had reached its end in Jesus the Christ. All four evangelists therefore knew that John the Baptist spoke the words with which the Second Isaiah opened his message as words that applied to the present. Those words of joy, light and comfort were for the writers of the Christian Gospels a present reality. The promise expressed by the Second Isaiah had been fulfilled in Christ.

Within this tradition that was common to all four Gospels, however, each of the evangelists expressed the special tradition of one local church with its particular emphasis on faith, prayer and interpretation. In this way, the one mystery of Jesus was disclosed in many different forms.

In what way was Luke different from the other evangelists? One example of his special emphasis can be seen in his quotation from the Second Isaiah, which is longer than that provided in the Gospels of Matthew or Mark, both of which contain this quotation. Luke included the words: "And all flesh shall see the salvation of God" (3:6), thus showing, at the very beginning of his Gospel, that he wanted to stress that the light of Jesus was shed on all peoples, that God's salvation was intended for all men and that each individual had the task of handing on that salvation. Luke's message, then, is that this God must be shared with others. He is properly addressed only when we call him "our" Father and when we all pray to him with the word "we," as all the children of God.

The solemn and ceremonial opening of this chapter of the Gospel of Luke, in which the place of Jesus Christ in the history of the known world is established and at the same time the history of Israel's salvation is inserted into the history of all men, should also be understood in this sense. Although Luke was concerned with the historicity of Jesus as opposed to the unhistorical nature of a mythical bringer of salvation, it was not his primary intention to demonstrate that we can visit the places that the historical Jesus visited, hold in our hands the coins that he touched, or read the scrolls that he knew. He showed the historicity of Jesus clearly enough, but he went further and pointed to the universality of Jesus. Jesus did not belong to one people. He belonged and still belongs to the *oikoumene*. Faith is the way for all people in the whole of the inhabited world. The time of Jesus—the time of the Church—is the time of mission. We can only believe with Jesus if our faith and our life are missionary and if we really want all flesh to see the salvation of God.

The meaning of Advent is also made clear in these words of joy, light and comfort. It is only when all flesh sees God that his coming will be complete. It is only when the new heaven and the new earth are there for everyone that they will exist. The aim of these words is to open the heart of Christianity—our own heart. We can only pray "thy kingdom come"—the Advent prayer that the Lord himself gave us—properly when we have let ourselves be changed by it: in other words, when we have let ourselves be made open by that prayer to all God's children: "All flesh shall see the salvation of God."

❧ PART II ❧

Reflections at Advent and Christmas

PREFACE

THE AIM of these three Advent and Christmas meditations is to stimulate that inner vision which gave rise to the Biblical truth: "The goodness and loving kindness of God our Savior [have] appeared" (Tit. 3:4). My three contributions to this little collection therefore clearly have the same intention as the last meditation, by the late Albino Luciani, the Cardinal and Patriarch of Venice, who became known to the world for a moment in time as Pope John Paul I. This "Lesson of the Christmas Donkey" is also included in memory of his gift to the world—his smile.

Joseph Cardinal Ratzinger
Munich, Feast of Francis of Assisi, 1978

I

At the Beginning of Advent

An Advent Conversation with the Sick

WHEN IT IS POSSIBLE to sense the quiet joy of the time just
before Christmas everywhere around us, it is in many ways particularly difficult to be ill and not to be able to experience the joy
of this season. But Advent may perhaps act in a very special way
as a medicine for the soul and make the forced inactivity and
suffering of illness more bearable. It may even help to reveal the
grace that is concealed in sickness.

I.

Let us just think for a moment what "Advent" means. It is a
Latin word that can be translated as "presence" or "coming."[1] In
the ancient world, it was a technical term, denoting the arrival
of a person in office such as a king or an emperor. It could also
indicate the coming of the deity, in which case the god's advent
was his emerging from concealment and making his presence

known in power or else having it solemnly celebrated in an act of worship.

Christians took over this word in order to express their particular relationship with Jesus Christ. For them, he was—and is—the king who has entered this wretched province, the earth, and enables it to celebrate his visit. He is the one whom they believe to be present when they meet together in liturgical celebration. What Christians meant—and still mean—in general by this word "Advent," then, is: God is there. He has not withdrawn from the world. He has not left us alone. Even though we cannot see him or touch him as we can the things that surround us, he is still there and, what is more, he comes to us in many different ways.

We have mentioned the word "visit" in this context. This word can be used in its happy, original and almost literal sense of "going to see" a person, persons or a place. It is, however, also used in the less pleasant sense of afflicting or punishing, when it is associated with such concepts as trouble, famine, plague or illness. This word should therefore enable us to see that something of the beauty of Advent can be found even in difficulty.

Illness and suffering can therefore, like a great joy, also be a personal Advent—a visit by God who wants to enter my life

---

1. See P. Jounel in A. G. Martimort, ed., *Handbuch der Liturgiewiessenschaft, II* (Freiburg i. Br., 1963), pp. 266–76; for the meaning of the word *adventus*, see also Blaise and Chirat, *Dictionnaire francais des auteurs chrètiens* (Turnhout, 1954), p. 61f.; for the history and theology of Advent, see J. Pascher, *Das liturgische Jahr* (Munich, 1963), pp. 332ff.

and turn toward me. However great our difficulties may be, we should always try to see our illness in this light and recognize that the Lord has interrupted our activity for a while in order to let us be quiet.

In my everyday life, I have very little time, both for him and for myself. I am completely harnessed to my activities from early in the morning until late at night—to such an extent, perhaps, that I even try to avoid myself because I do not know what to do with myself and am frightened of the encounter. My profession or work possesses me. Society possesses me. Pleasure has me in its grip. But I do not have myself. I gradually become, in the depths of my being, overgrown with weeds. I am driven along by things and other people, just a function in their ceaseless bustle.

Now, however, God has taken me out of this activity and I have to be quiet. I must wait. I must reflect about myself. I must bear being alone. I must bear pain and I must learn how to accept myself. It is difficult.

Is it true that God is waiting for me in this quietness? Is it not possible that he wants to do with me what the fourth Gospel says he does to the vine: "Every branch that does bear fruit he prunes, that it may bear more fruit" (John 15: 2)?

If I learn how to accept myself in this time of quietness and if I learn how to put up with pain and suffering in the knowledge that the Lord is "pruning" me, shall I not be much richer than if I had been earning a great deal of money? Is what is happening to me now not more fruitful and lasting than all the things—money and possessions—that can be counted and evaluated?

A visit from the Lord—illness can perhaps take on an entirely new appearance if we regard it as a kind of Advent. We do not rebel against our illness because it causes us to suffer pain or discomfort or even because being quiet and lonely is difficult. We rebel against it mainly because we ought to be doing so many important things and our forced idleness seems meaningless. But it is not at all meaningless. It has great significance within the structure of human life. It is possible for it to be God's moment in our life—the time when we are really open to him and when we can therefore learn how to find ourselves again.

Perhaps we should try to see each individual event in the day as a signal from God to us. Perhaps we should not simply take to heart all the irritating and unpleasant things, but take the trouble to find out how often God lets me perceive something of his love. We should, in other words, keep an inner diary of everything that is good each day. That would surely be a fine and saving task.

The Lord is there. This Christian certainly ought to help us to look at the world with different eyes and see that being visited by sickness is really being visited by him, a way in which he is able to come to us and be close to us.

II.

A second aspect of Advent is waiting, a waiting that is full of hope. In this, Advent enables us to understand the content and meaning of Christian time and of history as such. Jesus made this visible in many of the parables—in the story of the servants waiting for the return of their lord or forgetting and behaving as though they were the owners of the property; in the story of the bridesmaids waiting for or not being able to wait for the coming of the bridegroom; and in the parables of sowing and the harvest.

Man is always waiting in his life. As a child, he is waiting till he is grown up. As an adult, he wants to get on and be successful. Later, he longs for peace and quiet. Then finally the time comes when he discovers that he has had too little hope, when there is nothing left, beyond his work and position in life, to hope for.

Mankind has never been able to cease hoping for better times. Christians have always hoped that the Lord will always be present in history and that he will gather up all our tears and all our troubles so that everything will be explained and fulfilled in his kingdom.

It becomes especially clear during a time of illness that man is always waiting. Every day we are waiting for a sign of improvement and in the end for a complete cure. At the same time, however, we discover how many different ways there are of waiting.

When time itself is not filled with a present that is meaningful, waiting becomes unbearable. If we have to look forward to something that is not there now—if, in other words, we have nothing here and now and the present is completely empty, every second of our life seems too long. Waiting itself becomes too heavy a burden to bear, when we cannot be sure whether we really have anything at all to wait for.

When, on the other hand, time itself is meaningful and every moment contains something especially valuable, our joyful anticipation of the greater experience that is still to come makes what we have in the present even more precious and we are carried by an invisible power beyond the present moment. Advent helps us to wait with precisely this kind of waiting. It is the essentially Christian form of waiting and hoping.

The gifts of Jesus Christ are, after all, not purely future gifts—they reach into the present. Christ is invisibly present here and now. He speaks to me in many different ways in the present. He speaks to me through Holy Scripture, through the Church's year, through the saints, through everyday events, through the whole of creation. The world, when I am conscious of his presence in it, looks different than when it is obscured by the mist of an uncertain origin and an uncertain future. He speaks to me, but I can also speak to him. I can complain to him. I can present him with my sufferings, my impatience, and my questions, in the knowledge that he is always present and listening.

If he is there, time cannot be empty and meaningless. Every moment is valuable, even though I am incapable of doing anything but simply putting up with my sickness. If he exists, I can always hope, even though others can offer me no hope. Old age and retirement are not the final stages in life, from which one can only look backward. An even greater experience is still to come and a time that seems from the outside to be quite useless may be a time when we can achieve the highest form of maturity.

Time is not devalued by Christian hope. On the contrary, this hope means that every moment of our life has a special value. It means that we are able to accept the present and fill it, since everything that we have inwardly accepted remains.

III.

I have already hinted at the third aspect of Advent. It is not only a time of the present and a time of waiting for eternity—it is also in a very special sense a time of joy. What is more, it is a time of inner joy that cannot be driven out by suffering.

This can perhaps be understood best if we look closely at the inner content and meaning of our Advent practices. Almost all of these have their origin in Scripture, and the Church has used the words of Scripture in the season of Advent as prayers. The people of God have, as it were, translated Scripture into a visible form.

In Psalm 96, for example, we read: "Then shall all the trees of the wood sing for joy before the Lord, for he comes." In our Advent liturgy, these words have been joined to words from other psalms and the whole has been extended until we have: "Mountains and hills will sing praises before God and all the trees of the wood will clap their hands, for the Lord is coming, the ruler, to an eternal kingdom."

Our decorated Christmas trees are really nothing but an attempt to make these words visible. The Lord is there. Our ancestors believed this and the trees of the wood had therefore to go to meet him, bend down before him, and be a song of praise to their Lord. They believed this with such certainty too that the mountains and hills singing before the Lord became a living reality for them. They themselves broke into such a song of praise and it can still be heard today, so that we too have an inkling of the nearness of the Lord, since such sounds can be given to man only when the Lord is very close to him.

Even such an apparently external custom as our Christmas fare has its roots in the Church's Advent liturgy, which echoes the wonderful words of the Old Testament: "On that day the mountains will drip sweetness and the rivers will bring down milk and honey." It was in words such as these that men in the past expressed the quintessence of their hopes in a redeemed world and their thoughts were echoed by our ancestors when they celebrated Christmas as the time when God really came. If he comes at Christmas, he as it were distributes honey and it must therefore be true that the earth flows with it. Where he is, there can, after all, be no bitterness. In his presence, heaven and earth are in harmony and God and man are at one. Honey and all the sweet things of Christmas are the sign of this peace, concord and joy.

Christmas became the feast of giving, and in this we imitate the God who gives himself and also gives us life. This life itself becomes a gift when added to the milk of human existence, that one Love which cannot be threatened by death or unfaithfulness or deceit.[2]

All these elements come together in our joy that God became a child who encourages us to trust as children trust, to give ourselves, and to let ourselves receive.

---

2.   See J. Pieper, *About Love* (Chicago: Franciscan Herald Press, 1974), p. 28.

It is perhaps quite difficult for us to accept this joy when we are troubled by questions and when physical illness and spiritual problems attack us and make us rebel against the God we cannot understand. But this Child is a sign of hope and that sign is made on those who are in any way distressed. That is why it has been able to awaken such a pure echo that its power to console also touches the hearts of unbelievers.

Perhaps we ought to celebrate Advent by allowing the signs of this special time to penetrate freely into our hearts without resisting them in any way. We should also perhaps let ourselves be made warm by them without asking difficult questions and then, full of trust, accept the immeasurable goodness of the Child who made the mountains and hills sing and transformed the trees of the wood into a song of praise.

II

"And the Word Became Flesh"

A Christmas Sermon

IN THE GOSPEL of the third Mass of Christmas day (John 1:1–18), all that is familiar and lovable in the birth of Jesus Christ in the stable in Bethlehem seems to have been withdrawn into the strange sphere of mystery. It tells us nothing about the Child and his mother, the shepherds and their sheep or the song of the angels proclaiming peace to all men in the glory of God.

There is, however, something in it that is common to the other Gospel stories. Today's Gospel also speaks of light, shining in the darkness. It also speaks of the glory of God, visible to us as grace in the Word made flesh, and it speaks of the Lord, who was not received by his own people.

The stall in which the Son of David was born because there was no place for him in his own town suddenly becomes visible through the mysterious words of the Gospel; and if we listen at a deep enough level, it soon becomes clear that today's Gospel speaks only of the holy night of Christmas. We can therefore be sure that all the evangelists proclaim the same Gospel.

Luke and Matthew begin with the earthly story, and this opens the way into God's hidden activity. John, the eagle, looks out from the mystery of God and shows how this leads into the stable and, even deeper, into the flesh and blood of man.

What is involved here really? What does the Church really want to tell us about Christmas day, the whole year, and our own lives, in placing before us this solemn and strict text, when we would prefer to hear the warm words of the story of Jesus' birth?

I.

This Gospel has formed part of the liturgy of Christmas since earliest times, because it contains a statement which proclaims the real content of the feast and forms the basis of our joy—"the Word became flesh and dwelt among us" (John 1:14).

At Christmas, we are not celebrating the birthday of any great man of whom there are, as we know, so many. We are also not simply celebrating the mystery of childhood.

There can be no doubt that children can give us hope—they are pure, unused by the world and open—and courage to look for new human possibilities. But if we cling too much to the possibility of a new beginning in life that we see in children, we may have nothing at the end but sadness, since the newness of childhood can also be used by the world. Children also have eventually to enter the competitive battle of life and become compromised in it. They too have to be humiliated and in the end, like us all, fall victim to death.

If we had no more to celebrate at Christmas than simply an idyll of birth and childhood, how could we ever believe that it really is an idyll? After all, we are confronted by the perennial question of being born, becoming and dying. We are bound to ask whether it is not ultimately very sad to be born, since it inevitably leads only to death. But what happened here was much more than this—the Word became flesh.

What happened at Christmas was the birth of God's Son, something tremendous and beyond our imagination and reason, yet an event that had always been expected and was indeed necessary. What happened was that God entered our world and came among us. God and man became so inseparably united that this man was and is really God from God and light from light. He was and is true man.

The eternal meaning of the world came so close to us in this event that we can touch him with our hands and see him with our eyes (see 1 John 1:1). What John calls the "Word" is, after all, much more than this. In Greek thought of the period, it meant equally "meaning." It would therefore not be wrong to translate the sentence as: The meaning became flesh.

This meaning, however, is not simply a universal idea forming part of the world. It has turned toward us. It is a word, addressing us. It knows us, calls us, leads us. It is not a universal law in which we have some part to play. It is given in a completely personal way to each of us. It is itself a person—the Son of the living God, who was born in the stable at Bethlehem.

Many people—all of us to some degree—feel that this is too beautiful to be true. What we are told is that there is really a meaning. This meaning is, moreover, not simply an impotent protest against meaninglessness. The meaning has great power. It is God. And God is good.

God is not some distant, sublime being that we can never approach. He is very near, within calling distance, easy to reach. He has time for us—so much time that he lay in the crib as man and remained eternally man.

Again and again we ask: Is it possible? Is it suitable for God to be a child? The fact is that we are hardly able and do not want to believe that the truth is beautiful. In our own experience, it is, in the end, hard, cruel and dirty. Even when it really seems not to be so, we fret and worry so much about it that we are strengthened in our original conviction.

It used to be said that art was at the service of beauty and that beauty in art was the *splendor veritatis*: the inner shining of truth. Now, however, the task of art would seem to be to expose man as dirty and disgusting.

If we look at the plays of Brecht, for example, we cannot deny that his whole genius is turned toward the revelation of truth. He does not, however, try to show its inner shining. For him, dirt is truth. Contact with the truth does not make us noble. It lowers us. One consequence of this is that Christmas is mocked and joy is derided.

Indeed, if there is no God, then there is no light. There is only the dirt of the earth. This is the tragic truth of this kind of literature.

II.

"His own people received him not" (John 1:11). In the end, our own proud despair is preferable to us than the goodness of God, who, from the crib in Bethlehem, wants to touch our hearts. In the end, we are too proud to let ourselves be redeemed.

"His own people received him not." The depths of this statement are not fully plumbed in the story of the search for accommodation at an inn, which also forms part of games around the crib at Christmas. They are also not plumbed in the moral appeal to think of those who are homeless throughout the world and in our own towns and cities, however important this appeal may be. No, "his own people received him not" touches something even deeper in us all. It penetrates to the innermost reason why so many are homeless in the world—in our pride, we close the door on God and our fellowmen.

We are too proud to see God. We are like Herod and his theological specialists. At this level, we cannot hear the angels singing. At this level, we feel either threatened or bored by God. At this level, we do not want to belong to God—we only want to belong to ourselves. We do not want to be "his own property" and that is why we cannot receive the one who comes into his own property ("he came to his own home," John 1:11). To do this, we have to change and recognize him as the owner.

He came as a child to break through our pride. We might perhaps have capitulated more quickly if we had been confronted with power or even with wisdom. But he does not want our capitulation—he wants our love. He wants to set us free from our pride and in this way make us really free.

We should therefore let the joy of Christmas quietly penetrate into our hearts. It is not an illusion. It is the truth. And the truth—ultimate, real truth—is beautiful. It is also good. Encounter with it makes people good. It is the message of the Child who was God's own Son.

III.

Our passage ends with the statement: "We have beheld his glory…" (John 1:14). These may have been the words of the shepherds when they went home and tried to summarize their experience. They may have been the words of Mary and Joseph describing their memory of the night in Bethlehem. They are in fact the words of the disciple looking back and expressing what happened to him in his encounter with Jesus.

As Christians, we should really all be able to say these words with conviction: "We have beheld his glory." It is even possible to define faith on the basis of this statement—seeing his glory in this world.

If we believe, we can see. But have we really seen? Have we not simply remained blind? Do we not only go on seeing ourselves and our mirror-image? Each of us can only see outside himself what is in accordance with an inner reality.

Let us open our eyes to the mystery of Christmas. Let this mystery make us seeing, so that we shall be able to live looking at his glory, as people who do not simply think about and know only themselves. Let us respond positively to the call of Christmas. Let us learn how to see and hear and to receive him. Let us recognize God as the one who really owns us as "his own."

In this way, we can become ourselves bearers of the light that shines from Bethlehem and pray with confidence: May your kingdom come, may your light come, may your joy come. Amen.

III

The Lesson of the Christmas Donkey[†]

✦ *by* Pope John Paul I ✦

THE MOST HUMBLE of all the figures around the crib is the donkey. As a patriarch—the Patriarch of Venice—should I really say this to my readers? Do I cause offense? I hope not.

When I was very young, I was told that the little wooden fellow, Pinocchio, was punished by being changed into a donkey. A little later, I went to the theater and saw Ferravilla's *The Donkey Class*, the farce on which Massinelli based his cleverly written work. It was like a straight line consisting only of length and completely without breadth and depth. Its theme was in its refrain: "O what a beautiful feast!" Later still, discussing a judgment of our neighbor that was not in any sense exaggerated in its sensitivity, we often heard it said that a fellowman carried his brain on his back—in other words, he was a bit silly and was therefore a "donkey."

First published in *Il Gazzettino*, Venice (December 24, 1977).

Let us be honest. We have a prejudice against donkeys. Christ did not. For his entry into Jerusalem, he chose a gentle little ass. Francis Jammes, the Pascoli of France, praised donkeys most lovingly in his poems. Francis of Assisi often called his body Brother Ass, and when he was close to death he asked forgiveness of Brother Ass for having treated him so badly.

Donkeys are hard-working. Nowadays we do not see them so often as we did in the past. Then it was a common sight to see them with great baskets hanging down on each side or with so many battered pots on their backs. We often saw them pulling tightrope walkers' carts and indeed little carriages of all kinds. When I was a boy, I used to see donkeys with narrow trousers covering their skinny legs to protect the bleeding and discharging wounds from the flies that would otherwise have covered them in droves. The poorest donkeys went on pulling their carts in spite of everything!

All of us are told, in this time of great crisis, to go on pulling our carts instead of slinking off and leaving the office or the factory without an urgent reason. If we are really ill, we are allowed to stay at home, but it is a bad affair when imaginary illnesses or unreal injuries are covered with trousers or stockings that are really only quickly produced medical certificates or invented excuses which enable us to be away from our place of work.

A nation cannot get over a long, bad period without making sacrifices and working hard for a long time without strikes and labor unrest. The same applies to the world of education. There are demands for different kinds of schools at all levels, a more integrated program of learning, more comprehensive schools, more activities outside school and so on; and all kinds of experiments are being made, some good, some less good. Our modern educational institutions may well—and we hope they will—enable our pupils and students to learn more and study better. But if the whole of school and university life is disturbed by student demonstrations and protest marches? If the concept of diversity in the educational process is only used to let the pupils and students do nothing and the teaching staff lose themselves in talk? And if teachers and lecturers are so burdened with administrative tasks that they find it difficult or impossible to carry out their teaching duties?

The donkey has for centuries been the poor man's friend. According to a Greek legend, the devil has always worked against God, and as soon as God has succeeded in creating something the devil has always tried to bring about something else that would go against it. One day, he made a donkey, but he could not give it life, so he went to the Lord and said: "You give it life!" God did what he wanted, but he did it in his own way. "Get up, donkey," he said, "and from now on be the right arm of the little people!"

The legend goes on to describe what happened. The poor, who could not afford a horse or a mule, had a donkey. They loaded him with bundles of wood and he carried these home for them. They loaded him with corn and he carried it to the mill. They loaded him with dung and he carried it to the fields. They loaded him with everything…. The donkey was their best helper. Without him, they would have too hard a life.

How would it be if high-ranking people chose to be nothing else but little donkeys of the poor? Ignazio Silone tells a story from his youth which has made an unforgettable impression on me—the story of his meeting at the railway station with Don Luigi Orione. As a boy, he had to move from Rome into a college in Liguria. He observed an inconspicuous little priest who took charge of him and the other boys. Silone was annoyed because the famous Don Orione had not come himself. It seemed right that the little priest should carry his cases and bags and he did not stir to help him in any way.

When they were all sitting in the train, the priest asked him if he would like a newspaper. "Yes—the *Avanti*," Silone replied in a defiant voice. The priest got out of the train. When he returned, he gave the boy a copy *Avanti*.

Later, during the journey, Silone asked: "Why did Don Orione not come?" The priest replied: "I am Don Orione. I am sorry I did not introduce myself." Silone wrote: "I wanted the ground to open and swallow me up. I felt despicable and mean.... I stammered an apology for having let him carry my cases and bags. He smiled and confided in me that it gave him pleasure to be able to carry case sometimes for cheeky boys like me.... Then he made a further confidence: 'My vocation is to live as God's donkey,' he said."

It is good to remember this, especially nowadays, when there are so many poor people and also so many people who speak and write on behalf of the "disadvantaged," but so few who are real "donkeys" and ready to take other people's burdens on their backs.

For example, is not a great pity that there are families who could, without too much inconvenience, take in their elderly relatives instead of having them put into an old people's home? I know that it is the only possibility in many cases, but then the sons and daughters should remain close to their relatives, visit them as often as they can, and surround them with loving attention. It so often happens that their relatives hardly look after them at all and leave them alone with the pain of feeling that they are forgotten.

The Christmas donkey has another lesson to teach us—that of gentleness and patience. Just look at him. He stands with his head bowed and his feet together. It is very moving to see him! Even when he is attacked by hornets, wasps and gnats, his only defense is to twitch his long ears. He is the poorest of creatures, not equipped for the merciless battle that we have to fight if we are to obtain greater justice in the world. He is even less suited to live at a time when violence is the order of the day, when men deprive each other of their freedom, throw Molotov cocktails, write threatening letters, and talk incessantly of revolution. The little donkey would find it easier to understand a good mother getting her little daughter ready to go to school, wrapping up her books with colored paper, and taking her on the way. He would not, however, understand what was printed in those books: "Revolutions are a necessary consequence...when the proletariat, after decades of oppression, is ultimately driven to revolt.... We shall take up the cause of the proletariat."

These words are taken from a textbook for a senior class in Italian secondary schools. How similar they are—as alike as two eggs or two slices of the same apple—to the words that Lafayette spoke on February 20, 1790, to the French Constitutional Assembly: "Revolution is the most sacred of all duties." That uprising in fact took place and became known in history as the French Revolution. It solved many problems, created many others, and a great deal of blood was shed.

There was underground literature at that time, too, of the kind known nowadays as "samizdat." One secretly published document that sold particularly well was a little book entitled *Reflections about France* by Joseph de Maistre. In 1796 alone it was reprinted three times. In it were these words: "No despot has ever played with the lives of a people as the Jacobins do now and no people has ever let itself be slaughtered so passively.... After the Revolution had punished the monarchy and the aristocracy for their sins, it swallowed itself.... Eighteen Superiors of religious institutes were sent to the guillotine, eight were deported, and six were incarcerated. Seventy members of religious institutes were sent to the guillotine and one hundred and thirty were deported."

The Revolution had begun with the best of intentions. The slogan that was used throughout was: "Liberty, equality, fraternity." But the dam was breached and nothing could hold back the flood waters. Jeanne Roland, a champion of the Revolution, understood this only too well. It did not help her in any way that her husband was a minister of state. The people did not even allow her to defend herself at the tribunal, because, although she was a revolutionary, she was a moderate Girondist. Condemned by the Jacobins, she was led to the scaffold. On her way, she bowed before the statue of liberty and cried out: "O Liberty, how many crimes have been committed in your name!"

Let us, in conclusion, return to the little donkey and to Francis Jammes, French Christian poet, who sang his praises. In a prayer asking to be allowed to enter paradise with the donkeys, he wrote: "If I ever come to you, my God, I will take my staff and say to my friends the donkeys on the highroad: 'Come with me, poor beasts.' I would like to appear before you, my God, surrounded by these animals I love so much."

I would not go so far as to say this. It would be enough for me to enter heaven along the way that I would like to learn from Jesus, his and my mother, the saints and—why not, if it is of help?—the humble little donkey at the crib.

PART III

The Contribution of St. Francis to Christmas

THE CONTRIBUTION
OF ST. FRANCIS
TO CHRISTMAS

CHRISTENDOM'S PRIMARY FEAST is not Christmas but Easter: the Lord's resurrection constituted the initial breakthrough of a new life, and so was the beginning of the Church. Ignatius of Antioch (at the latest A.D. 117) describes Christians, therefore, as those who "no longer keep the sabbath, but live by the Day of the Lord."[1] To be a Christian means to live in Easter joy, having one's life oriented toward the Resurrection, which is celebrated in the weekly Easter festival that is Sunday.

I. *Jesus' Birthday on December 25*

The first to affirm that Jesus was born on December 25 was, without doubt, Hippolytus of Rome, in his commentary on Daniel, written in about the year 204. Bo Reicke, a scholar in Basel, believes that there are certain indications from which he can prove that St. Luke the Evangelist had already presupposed that December 25 was the birthday of Jesus. His argument runs thus. This was the day on which the feast of the Dedication of the Temple, inaugurated in 164 B.C. by Judas Maccabeus, was celebrated. The date of Christ's birth, his coming, the light of God rising in the darkness of winter, would therefore at the same time symbolize the real dedication of the Temple—the arrival of God upon this earth.

However that may be, not until the fourth century did the feast of Christmas acquire a distinct shape in the Church. In that period it supplanted the Roman festival of *Sol Invictus* and presented the birth of Christ as the victory of the true light. Bo Reicke's observations have made it clear, that ancient Judeo-Christian traditions were caught up in this adaptation of the pagan festival to become a major Christian feast.

II. *The Special Warmth We Feel in the Feast of Christmas*

This warmth was not generated until the Middle Ages, and it was St. Francis of Assisi, with his tremendous devotion to *God-with-us*, who contributed so much to the development of this new dimension.

1. His first biographer, Thomas of Celano, recounts the following in his second account of Francis' life. "More than any other feast, it was Christmas that he celebrated with an indescribable joy. He said that was the feast of all feasts, for on this

---

1.   Ignatius of Antioch, *Letter to the Magnesians*, 9.

day God became a little child. With what tenderness and devotion Francis embraced pictures of the Child Jesus, stammering like a child, with great compassion, words full of tenderness! On his lips the name of Jesus was sweet as honey."[2]

2. Out of such sentiments emerged the famous celebration of Christmas at Greccio, to which he may have been motivated by his visit to the Holy Land and to the crib at Santa Maria Maggiore in Rome. The decisive thing that motivated him was his longing for nearness, for reality—the desire to be really present in Bethlehem, to experience directly the joy of the birth of the Child Jesus, and to share all of this with all his friends. Celano's account, in the first biography, of this night at the crib has the power of a perpetual stimulus to men in all ages, and has been the determining factor in enabling this most beautiful Christmas custom—the crib—to develop.

3. There is one event of this night that seems to be worth special mention. The land around Greccio had been put at the disposal of the poor by a nobleman called John. Celano tells us that despite his aristocratic origin and his important position, this man "set no store by nobility of blood, but aspired to that of the soul." Because of this, Francis loved him.[3] According to Celano, during that night the grace of a wonderful vision was granted to John. He saw lying motionless in the manger a little Child who was roused from sleep at the approach of Francis.

2. II Celano, CLI, 199.
3. I Celano, XXX, 84.

"This vision corresponded exactly to what was happening in reality, for the Child was indeed asleep in the forgetfulness of hearts. And then, through his servant Francis, memory was awakened and indelibly imprinted in the mind."[4]

III. *The New Dimension*

This picture describes very exactly the new dimension that Francis—his faith infusing heart and mind—gave to the Christian festival of Christmas. It was the discovery of the revelation of God that lies precisely in the Child Jesus. In this very manner God truly became "Emmanuel," God-with-us, not in the least separated from us by any height or distance.

1. As a child he has come so close to us that we can speak to him, unembarrassed, in the language we would use to any baby.

2. In the Child Jesus is demonstrated with the utmost clarity the defenselessness of the love of God. God comes without weapons, because he desires to conquer not from without but from within, through an interior transformation. If there is anything at all that is able to conquer man's self-will, his violence, his greed, it is the defenselessness of the child. God has assumed this quality so as to conquer us and lead us to himself.

3. We must not forget, however, that the highest title given to Jesus Christ is "the Son"—the Son of God. The divine dignity is expressed in a word that proclaims Jesus as forever the Son.

---

4. I Celano, XXX, 86.

His being a child bears a unique correspondence to his divinity, which is the divinity of "the Son." Thus his being a child is the pointer for us to the way along which we can become divinized. This is what makes sense of his saying, "Unless you turn [i.e., *are converted*] and become like children you will never enter the kingdom of heaven" (Matt. 18:3). He who has not grasped the mystery of Christmas, has not grasped the distinguishing quality of being a Christian. He who has not assumed this quality cannot enter the kingdom of heaven. This is what St. Francis wanted to imprint upon the mind of Christendom in his own time—and in all succeeding ages.

IV. *The Ox and the Ass at the Crib*

On St. Francis' instructions, on the holy night there stood in the cave at Greccio an ox and an ass. He had said to John the nobleman: "I would like to arouse the memory of the Child with all possible realism, just as he was born in Bethlehem, with all the hardship that he had to suffer in his childhood. I would like to see him with my bodily eyes, lying in a manger, asleep on the hay, between an ox and an ass."[5] Since then the ox and the ass have been part of every crib. But where did they really come from?

1. We all know that the New Testament narratives about Christmas contain no mention of these creatures. If we pursue

---

5.   I Celano, XXX, 84.

this question we come upon facts that are important for the whole range of Christmas observance, and, indeed, for the Christmas and Easter practice of the Church, in the liturgy as well as in popular devotion.

2. The ox and the ass are not mere products of pious imagination. They have become companions to the Christmas scene as a result of the Church's belief in the unity of the Old and the New Testament. In Isaiah 1:3 we read: "The ox knows its owner, and ass its master's crib. But Israel has no knowledge, my people does not understand." In these words the Fathers of the Church saw a prophetic utterance that pointed toward the new people of God, the Church, comprising both Jews and pagans.

3. In God's sight, all men, Jews and pagans, like oxen and asses, were without understanding and knowledge. But the Child in the crib had opened their eyes, so that now they recognized the voice of their owner, the voice of their master. It is striking how the medieval representations of the Christmas event again and again portray both animals with almost human faces, as they stand and bow with reverence and understanding before the mystery of this Child. With understanding, for both animals are seen as the prophetic code behind which the mystery of the Church lies hidden—the mystery that is ourselves, who in the presence of the eternal are oxen and asses—oxen and asses whose eyes are opened in this holy night, so that they recognize their Lord in the crib.

But do we really recognize him? When we place the ox and the ass in the crib, we must call to mind the whole of Isaiah's affirmation, which is not only a gospel—promise of future recognition, but also a judgment upon present blindness. Ox and ass know "but Israel has no knowledge, my people does not understand."

V. *Who Are the "Ox and Ass" Who Recognize the Lord?*

Who are the ox and the ass today? Who are "my people"? Why is it that lack of understanding recognizes, while understanding is blind? To find an answer we must return with the Fathers of the Church to the first Christmas. Who failed to recognize; who did recognize; and why was it so?

1. The one who did not recognize was Herod; nor did he comprehend anything when told about the Child. He merely became increasingly blinded by his own lust for power with its associated persecutory paranoia (Matt. 2:3). "All Jerusalem with him" did not recognize either (ibid). Another group who did not recognize were the people "clothed in soft raiment" (Matt. 11:8)—the refined folk. And the learned, the masters of Scripture, the specialists in Scripture exegesis, who knew exactly the right passages of Scripture, but understood nothing—they did not recognize either (cf. Matt. 2:6).

2. Those who did recognize were—compared with the above celebrated people—"the ox and the ass": that is the shepherds, the Magi, Mary and Joseph. Could it be otherwise? In the stall, where we find him, refined folk do not feel at home, but only the ox and the ass.

3. And where do we fit in? Do we find ourselves far away from the stall, because we are too refined and too clever? Do we, too, not get so entangled in scholarly Scripture exegesis, in exposing what is unauthentic, in establishing the true historical setting, that we have become blind to the Child himself and fail to perceive anything of him at all? Are we not so firmly imprisoned in "Jerusalem," in Herod's palace, shut up in ourselves, in our self-will, our fear of persecution, that we are unable to hear the angel voices in the night and go and worship? And so, in this night, the faces of ox and ass gaze at us inquiringly: "My people does not understand; can you comprehend the voice of your Lord?" When we set up the familiar figures in the crib, we ought to implore the Lord to give our hearts the simplicity that discovers the Lord in the Child—as once did Francis in Greccio. That could happen to us too, what Celano—echoing the words of St. Luke concerning the shepherds on the first Christmas night (Luke 2:20)—tells us happened to those who took part in Matins at Greccio: everyone went home full of joy.[6]

---

6.   I Celano, XXX, 86.

CLUNY MEDIA

Designed by Fiona Cecile Clarke, the CLUNY MEDIA *logo depicts a monk at work in the scriptorium, with a cat sitting at his feet.*

The monk represents our mission to emulate the invaluable contributions of the monks of Cluny in preserving the libraries of the West, our striving to know and love the truth.

The cat at the monk's feet is Pangur Bán, from the eponymous Irish poem of the 9th century. The anonymous poet compares his scholarly pursuit of truth with the cat's happy hunting of mice. The depiction of Pangur Bán is an homage to the work of the monks of Irish monasteries and a sign of the joy we at Cluny take in our trade.

"Messe ocus Pangur Bán,
cechtar nathar fria saindan:
bíth a menmasam fri seilgg,
mu memra céin im saincheirdd."